The Manager as Change Leader

**Recent Titles in
The Manager as...**

The Manager as Politician
Jerry W. Gilley

The Manager as Mentor
Michael J. Marquardt and Peter Loan

The Manager as Change Leader

Ann Gilley

The Manager as. . .
Jerry W. Gilley, Series Editor

Westport, Connecticut
London

Library of Congress Cataloging-in-Publication Data

Gilley, Ann Maycunich.
  The manager as change leader—Ann Gilley.
    p. cm.—(The manager as..., ISSN 1555-7480)
  Includes bibliographical references and index.
  ISBN 0-275-98597-0 (alk. paper)
  1. Leadership. 2. Organizational change. 3. Management. I. Title. II. Series.
  HD57.7.G53   2005
  658.4′06—dc22   2005020498

British Library Cataloguing in Publication Data is available.

Library of Congress Catalog Card Number: 2005020498

ISBN: 0-275-98597-0

ISSN: 1555-7480

First published in 2005

Praeger Publishers, 88 Post Road West, Westport, CT 06881
An imprint of Greenwood Publishing Group, Inc.
www.praeger.com

Printed in the United States of America

The paper used in this book complies with the
Permanent Paper Standard issued by the National
Information Standards Organization (Z39.48-1984).

10 9 8 7 6 5 4 3 2 1

Contents

Publisher's Note   vii

PART I
Principles and Practices

1 Overview of Change   3

2 The Nature of Change   17

3 Roles and Responsibilities of a Change Leader   39

4 Skills and Competencies of a Change Leader   57

PART II
Action Plan, Tools, and Resources

5 Self-Assessment and Development 83

6 Tools for Success 97

7 Resources for the Manager as Change Leader 119

Notes 127
Index 131

Publisher's Note

The backbone of every organization, large or small, is its managers. They guide and direct employees' actions, decisions, resources, and energies. They serve as friends and leaders, motivators and disciplinarians, problem solvers and counselors, partners and directors. Managers serve as liaisons between executives and employees, interpreting the organization's mission and realizing its goals. They are responsible for performance improvement, quality, productivity, strategy, *and* execution through the people who work for and with them. All too often, though, managers are thrust into these roles and responsibilities without adequate guidance and support. MBA programs provide book learning but little practical experience in the art of managing projects and people; at the other end of the spectrum, exceptional talent in one's functional area does not necessarily prepare the individual for the daily rigors of supervision. This series is designed to address those gaps directly.

The Manager as... series provides a unique library of insights and information designed to help managers develop a portfolio of outstanding skills. From Mentor to Marketer, Politician to Problem Solver, Coach to Change Leader, each book provides an introduction to the principles, concepts, and issues that define the role; discusses the evolution of recent and current trends; and guides the reader through the dynamic process of assessing his or her strengths and weaknesses and creating a personal development plan. Featuring diagnostic tools, exercises, checklists, case examples, practical tips, and recommended resources, the books in this series will help readers at any stage in their careers master the art and science of management.

PART I

Principles and Practices

ONE

Overview of Change

Change is constant.

—Benjamin Disraeli

The vice president of accounting for a large firm decided to purchase a new, more user friendly automated accounting software program. Staff complaints regarding inefficiency and delays had reached the breaking point. The seven members of the department were notified two weeks prior to installation of the new software of the impending change, along with mandatory staff training. The atmosphere during the training session was toxic and failed to improve when employees returned to their desks. Productivity declined and tensions rose. The vice president was stunned. He had given his employees what they asked. What went wrong?

Change. That inevitable yet critical component of organizational life that causes frustration, stress, and ulcers due to opportunities, layoffs, downsizing, rightsizing, outsourcing, reengineering, mergers, acquisitions, sell-offs, promotions, demotions, transfers, hiring, firing... the list goes on and on. Countries, governments, communities, businesses, and individuals are in a constant state of change. How is a mere manager to cope?

THE TROUBLE WITH CHANGE

We live in challenging times, no doubt. Management is not for the faint of heart. Employees are asked to do more with less as their managers and leaders are challenged to inspire, motivate, and propel their departments into the next century. Ultimately, managers are responsible for implementing leadership's vision and strategy—making it happen. As a result, the essence of managerial practice is change. Managers help their people and organizations proceed from the here and now to the future, along a path illuminated by the vision, mission, and strategy. How are managers doing? Consider the following information on change:

- One-half to two-thirds of major corporate change initiatives are deemed failures.[1]
- Less than 40 percent of change efforts produced positive change.[2]
- One-third of major change efforts actually make the situation worse.[3]
- Less than 50 percent of reengineering programs are considered successes, some say less than 20 percent.[4]
- Many companies are finding that they must undertake moderate organizational changes at least once a year, and major changes every four or five years.[5]

Statistics such as these on the success rates of change are frightening. Undaunted, evolving legislation, globalization, technology, and society force organizations to constantly change. Success in organizational life will increasingly depend on one's ability to effectively implement change. Competitive pressures will drive it. So, too, will corporate strategy, shareholders, and customers. Successful managers understand that their role is to help the company remain competitive and grow—in short, continuous improvement brought about through change.

PURPOSE OF CHANGE

The accelerating pace of change means that being responsive to current customer needs and competitive pressures isn't enough—individuals and their companies must anticipate and prepare for future changes. The primary purpose of change is to improve the organization and make it more competitive, whether this is a large, total system or a small division or department within a firm. "Successful companies have succeeded by changing in ways that unleashed new sources of competitive advantage."[6]

Those individuals and firms able to adapt to, anticipate, or drive change prove more viable in the long term. Organizations unable to embrace change often face operational and financial difficulties that stem from the inability to remain flexible and adaptive to dynamic business environments. The inability to cope with change has been the demise of many firms over the years. Mergers, for example, are prime examples of largely unsuccessful efforts at change. Research indicates that more than one-third of large-scale change efforts, including mergers, don't work or even make the situation worse.[7] Continuous, rapid change significantly impacts the way organizations are managed, how they function, and their ability to remain competitive. Consequently, it is in a manager's best interests to understand the concepts of change and master the skills necessary to lead change within his or her department and organization.

MANAGEMENT VERSUS LEADERSHIP

Making change successfully happen requires a combination of a complex set of skills. Managers are often credited with implementation capabilities. They are seen as the evaluators, schedulers, and executors of policy and procedures, while concurrently interacting with frontline employees. Successful change efforts, however, begin with a vision embodied by a catalyst—someone who is able to inspire individuals as well as groups, build and motivate allies, and create synergy around a common goal.

A recent poll of workers by Maritz Research found that 21 percent of respondents would gladly fire the person in charge. The reasons cited include low job satisfaction, lack of respect workers receive from management, and management's failure to set a positive tone for workplace behavior and the overall work environment. Many managers focus on superficial activities and short-term results, profits, and stock prices. Too few have emerged as leaders who inspire, encourage innovation, create a healthy business culture, and focus on long-term goals.

Effective managers are not necessarily good leaders, and vice versa, yet both are critical components of successful organizations. The two involve completely different skill sets. Leadership entails vision along with the ability to inspire and motivate people to superior performance. Management brings the vision to reality by implementing the day-to-day operations of the firm. Few managers understand this fundamental difference. In fact, a midlevel manager at a large Midwest firm recently shared the following observation:

Within our organization it is assumed that, if you move up, you are a good leader—even if you are clearly in a managerial capacity. This approach simply breeds arrogance where it is not warranted. In my opinion, at least half of these people aren't leadership material.

Management and leadership are both vitally important. Highlighting the need for effective leadership does not minimize the importance of management, managers, or supervisors. Leadership simply involves unique skills and processes that are distinguishable from basic management practices: leadership charts the course (strategic) while management steers the vessel (operational).

When speaking on the topic of management versus leadership, I often begin the session by asking participants to describe well-known or famous leaders, their personality or behavioral characteristics, and specific responsibilities. Common responses include Theodore Roosevelt, George S. Patton, Abraham Lincoln, Winston Churchill, and Jesus Christ. Typical traits include visionary, driven, charismatic, inspiring, motivating, creative, and so forth. Responsibilities are to set a course to achieve the vision, create alliances, and inspire action, to name a few. Next, participants are asked to identify well-known or famous managers. The typical response? Stunned silence. Managers rarely achieve fame for their deeds—even though their actions are critical to the success of the venture. Leadership, being much more visible, engenders notoriety. The term *management* often carries a negative connotation, prompting visions of controlling, sometimes manipulative number crunchers more concerned about figures, policies, and processes than people or genuine results. Table 1.1 illustrates some differences between managers and leaders.

Table 1.1
Managers versus Leaders

Managers	Leaders
"Push" things (budgets, schedules, processes, procedures)	"Pull" people
Preserve the status quo	Challenge the status quo
Look down and in	Look up and out
Administer	Innovate
Maintain	Develop
Control	Inspire
Plan	Guide
Direct	Coach
Organize	Influence
Schedule	Facilitate

Table 1.2
Leadership and Management Impacts on Change

CULTURE			
EFFECTIVE (genuine leadership)	INPUTS	PROCESSING	OUTPUTS
	Data Information Communication	Involvement 2-way feedback Support Resources Rewards	Commitment Action Change
INEFFECTIVE (traditional management)	Management decisions	Directives Threats Coercion	Resentment Fear Failed change efforts
CULTURE			

Table 1.1 implies that people can be lead, but not managed. The same may be true for change. We respond favorably to persuasion, support, and effective communications, and negatively to force, threats, and lack of involvement. An organization's response to change both drives and is influenced by its culture, as illustrated by Table 1.2.

Management

The management function occurs at all levels within a firm, from frontline supervisors to midlevel managers to senior executives. Management is "the process of working with and through others to achieve organizational objectives."[8] Regardless of title or position within an organization, the traditional definition of management is *planning, directing, organizing, and controlling.* Planning involves systematically making decisions about the goals and activities that an individual, group, work unit, or the organization will pursue. Planning activities include analyzing, forecasting, setting objectives, allocating resources, crafting strategies, and determining activities in which the organization will engage to achieve its goals.

Directing is determining and communicating specific actionable plans to meet goals and objectives. Organizing entails assembling and coordinating the resources (human, financial, physical, informational, and other) and activities needed to achieve goals. Organizing includes specifying job responsibilities, scheduling work assignments, grouping jobs into work units, and creating conditions for people to achieve success.

The controlling function ensures that goals are met by monitoring progress and comparing actual outcomes to goals.

Contemporary Management

The traditional view of management, driven by a rapidly changing world, has evolved to include new dimensions of performance and behavioral expectations. Employees are demanding that their managers exhibit a wide range of competencies as opposed to mere technical skills. More and more, accepted definitions of management include expectations of leadership.[9] Superior performance depends on it.

Leadership

True leaders inspire us to make their vision our own, complete with requisite fervor and dedication. Leaders have the unique ability to make us feel good about ourselves and the choices we make. We choose to follow a leader to a place we would not go on our own, potential risk and all. Leaders build bridges and encourage us to follow them from today to tomorrow.

Why is leadership so important, and why now? The rapidly changing world in which we live, coupled with recent misdeeds and scandals at the executive level, makes for a crisis situation. At a time when leadership is most important—globally, competitively, even politically—we find that genuine leadership is indeed rare. Too often, those in power abuse that power for personal gain and at the expense of those who work for and with them. Employees, customers, shareholders, society, and change efforts suffer. Absent effective leadership, employees and their organizations fall short of expected performance.

Change Leadership

Change management usually focuses on implementation of a multistep change model designed to allow the process of change to flow smoothly. Change leadership, on the other hand, emphasizes the nature of the change and potential human responses to it. Leaders understand the complex psychology associated with change, along with the resultant need to build alliances and support and to channel passion and creativity—in short, whip people to an emotional peak. Charisma, enthusiasm, and an understanding of basic human motivators prove powerful skills.

Change leaders help their firms achieve a long-term competitive advantage by engaging in activities that support strategic initiatives. A leader of change is ready, willing, and able to *envision, inspire,* and *support* change necessary to move the organization forward.

Envision change: understand the critical need for altering the current state, imagine the future, and think outside the box with respect to the desired state and alternative approaches to get there.

Inspire change: actively sell the need for change, campaign and involve others, begin the process of change, and keep the momentum going.
Support change: secure resources for change, communicate with employees at all levels throughout the process, encourage and reward individual and group/team change efforts, be its biggest advocate.

Successful leaders of change possess a unique set of skills and abilities (see chapter 3) that enable their success. Fortunately, they are not alone. In fact, successful change efforts require a great deal of time, effort, and commitment from organizational players. Let's take a look at how organizations, collectively, deal with change.

ORGANIZATIONS AND CHANGE

Although many organizations and their leaders desire lasting, meaningful change, few are capable of achieving it. Individuals and their organizations often go through the motions necessary to bring about change while simultaneously hoping that its catalyst disappears. Why? Quite simply, change is disruptive—it upsets the balance with which we are comfortable. Change introduces an element of uncertainty, forcing us to face the unknown. And yet, change occurs so frequently, so continuously, that it is predictable to a large degree. It *will* happen—the question is when? How? And what will be the consequences? Fortunately, we have some control over when, how, and the results. The key lies in understanding change and human reactions to it.

Organizations are simply collections of people. Therefore, organizations, like people, are living systems. As such, they often react to change in ways that are irrational or unexpected. Organizational change efforts are influenced by individual and collective experiences, history, perceptions, and biases, and are further complicated by group processes, influences, pressures, and agendas. The high rate of organizational change failure is powerful testimony to the complexity of change and challenges faced by managers and employees. To better understand our potential for managing change, let's first look at the problems often associated with change efforts.

Problems with Change

Why is change so difficult? The reasons are many and varied, based on both individual and organizational perceptions, experiences, mistakes, and successes. A few common reasons are as follows:

- The change is ill-conceived (e.g., seen as a quick fix, as a solution to a symptom—not to the true problem, or as a solution in search of a problem).

- No one is in charge or accountable.
- The change is poorly implemented (e.g., lacks structure, details, resources, etc.).
- Few organizations take the time before a change to identify who might resist and why.
- Even changes considered positive involve loss and uncertainty.
- Supervisors/managers frequently attempt to make changes in employees when, in fact, the real need may be for a change in the system.
- Managers and executives are often powerful resistors while employees are usually blamed.
- Employees typically aren't involved until the implementation stage, not the decision-making stage.
- Individuals are inherently resistant to change (see chapter 2).
- Few leaders or managers understand the true complexities of change and the human reaction to it.
- The change is conceived, implemented, and managed from a purely technical viewpoint and without understanding of the human influence on its success or failure.
- The change-initiative team isn't communicating appropriately.

Implications for Managers

Most change efforts encounter problems. The results? Morale often falls or may be completely destroyed. Managers and employees become exhausted from the intensity of the efforts and related emotional upheaval. The change effort exceeds estimated time and budgeted costs. Strategic goals are not met. Conflict between and among employees rises. The list goes on. If not addressed, disaster may loom. To survive, managers must invoke a complex set of skills (e.g., motivation techniques, conflict-negotiation skills, high-level communications, and so forth; see chapter 4) to overcome these problems and move forward.

Failed change efforts may yield painful, costly consequences, including

- lower morale
- productivity losses
- loss of respect and/or trust for leaders/managers
- higher stress and levels of exhaustion
- cost overruns
- conflict, anger
- failure to meet personal, departmental, and organizational goals
- lower propensity to engage in future change efforts

Further complicating the subject of change are the numerous obstacles managers and employees face on a daily basis. They are discussed next.

Barriers to Change

The importance of change and its relationship to organizational viability is well known, yet occasionally change simply does not work. Unfocused, unplanned, or superficial change serves as a cotton candy approach to addressing real operational difficulties. Although individuals and organizations recognize the need for change, few are able to sustain successful change efforts.

A number of barriers prevent leaders, managers, employees, and organizations from successfully implementing long-term, systemic change. Some of the most common barriers to change include, but are not limited to

- inherent human resistance to change
- inability or unwillingness to deal with resistance when it occurs
- lack of skills and abilities (manager and employee) necessary to effectively implement change
- organizational immune system
- poor leadership
- short-term leadership
- failure to understand effective change-implementation techniques
- lack of management support for change
- lack of trust between management and employees
- internal conflict for resources, recognition, or rewards
- organizational overconfidence
- lack of critical reflective skills (the ability to examine current and past performance)
- lack of commitment to change
- lack of agreed-upon organizational vision, mission, and strategy
- differing organizational values
- lack of a payoff for change
- maintaining faulty assumptions related to change
- dysfunctional culture
- lack of consequences for inadequate or poor performance

First and foremost is our inherent resistance to change. People often view change as something to be feared. It may be disruptive, uncomfortable, or threatening to our security. Even change positioned as positive is often resisted in favor of what is comfortable and known. Our innate aversion to change at the individual, or micro, level impacts our behavior in groups/teams and organizationally, where we also block change efforts. Employee resistance is one of the most frequently cited problems associated with change implementation. Consider the times you were part of (or attempted to lead) a group whose efforts to improve, redesign, create, or problem solve met pointed resistance and/or proved frustrating. Individual reactions to change often manifest themselves, or are even compounded, when confronted by multiple colleagues who may be perceived as threats. The human reaction to change is discussed in greater detail in chapter 2.

Resistance to change at the macro, or organizational, level is represented by the organizational immune system. The human body utilizes certain cells as part of the immune system to protect it from harmful diseases, bacteria, or intrusions (e.g., slivers). Like the human body, organizations are protected from perceived threats by their own sentinels—people and procedures—who formally or informally shield their department or the firm from intrusions (e.g., ideas, initiatives) considered harmful. These individuals are found at all levels of the organization and may hold any position. They can be recognized by their negative perception of change, desire to protect the status quo, longing for the "good old days," and lack of engagement in discussions or actions that involve risk or the unknown. Understanding and dealing effectively with the organizational immune system is discussed in greater detail in chapter 2.

Leadership proves critical to the success of change efforts. Leaders and managers must visibly support the change, understand effective change-implementation techniques, and reward individuals, groups, and the organization for meeting change goals. Unfortunately, many firms attempt to implement long-term change initiatives with short-term leadership. Or, short-term or quick-fix changes are mandated in order to satisfy short-term shareholder expectations or guarantee leaders' annual bonuses. Actions such as these undermine trust for management and contribute to a dysfunctional culture devoid of its ability to sustain lasting, meaningful change. Change fails when leaders fail to lead, are afraid of the unknown, are unable to mobilize commitment to sustain change, allow political uncertainty to undermine necessary change, or when management neglects to generate tangible results. Ultimately, management is responsible for making change happen; therefore, managers must be held accountable for their performance and that of their employees.

Sometimes change does not bring about desired change.[10] Occasionally, expectations are simply not realistic because of limited individual talent and capabilities, resource constraints, or faulty assumptions (e.g., change will be easy). I worked with the newly appointed director of a marketing development department who had altered the incentive plan that had been in place for approximately three years. After abandoning the incentives based on premiums generated by each individual marketing representative in favor of a plan based on number of account calls made, performance (premiums) declined drastically in the first week and continued to fall steadily thereafter. Marketing representatives rebelled, some stating they felt demotivated and insulted by the new plan. What went wrong? The director had overlooked the fact that division and corporate goals were based on premium revenues, not calls made. He also failed to understand basic human motivation, desire for involvement in decision making, and subtle (and not-so-subtle) feedback.

Keep in mind that organizations are simply collections of people. Therefore, in order for the organization to change, its people—along with their attitudes, behaviors, responses, routines, and ways of accomplishing work—must change. So, what is a busy manager to do? Obstacles to change are numerous and varied, as are suggestions for overcoming them. Some of these are examined next.

Overcoming Barriers to Change

Barriers to change are as personal as the individual and as potentially complex as the organization. Overcoming barriers to change, then, requires knowing the individual on a personal level and an in-depth understanding of the firm, including its culture, management practices, propensity to change, procedures, capabilities, and weaknesses. The following list is by no means all-inclusive, nor does it guarantee change will occur in the desired manner. Employing these strategies will, however, increase your chances for success if you are able to determine what the change means from the employee's perspective and react accordingly. Some employees will need information or resources; others may need convincing. As a manager and champion of change, you should follow the strategies as shown in Table 1.3.

Despite our best intentions, change initiatives do not always proceed or end favorably. David Nadler said it well:

> The truth is that change is inherently messy. It is always complicated. It invariably involves a massive array of sharply conflicting demands. Despite the best-laid plans, things never happen in exactly the right order—and in fact, few things rarely turn out exactly right the first time around. Most important, the reality of change in the organizational trenches defies rigid academic models as well as superficial management fads.[11]

All we can do is our best. Armed with information, insight, and a little bit of luck, we can navigate the turbulent waters of change and hope to reach our desired destination.

WHAT'S NEXT?

This book is designed to help managers hone their skills as champions of change by incorporating change leadership into their skill set. Chapter 2 examines the heart of change in greater detail, offering definitions and

Table 1.3
Champion of Change Responsibilities

Determine what should be changed: strategy, structure, culture, systems, or people.	Make certain the focus of change is appropriate; too often we attempt to change the behavior of people when, in fact, the problem lies somewhere in the system.
Create a context for change.	Help employees understand why the change is needed, who it will benefit, and how and what will happen if we don't change.
Empathize; put yourself in your employees' shoes.	Based on your knowledge of each employee, how will he/she be impacted? How will he/she react and why? Which fears are logical, which are not? What coping skills does he/she possess?
Model the change.	Honestly support and champion the change; live it.
Remove obstacles in the system.	Identify and eliminate barriers embedded within organizational policies, practices, and procedures.
Understand that resistance is a valuable passion that can be channeled more constructively.	Identify and address reasons for an individual's resistance; engage him or her around that area.
Involve people at all levels in the change.	Involvement and participation lead to commitment. Identify strengths needed to make the change happen, and involve those who possess needed skills where appropriate. We support what we help create.
Communicate, communicate, communicate.	Provide those impacted by the change with sufficient information on a routine basis. Encourage questions and feedback.
Provide support.	Be enthusiastic of the change and supportive of employees being challenged to master new ways of business; provide resources; allow mistakes; protect / defend your people when necessary.

**Table 1.3
(continued)**

Recognize and reward employees' efforts.	Understand that change is difficult; recognize and reward individuals / groups / departments for their efforts.
Be firm when appropriate.	In spite of your best efforts, some personalities simply cannot accept change. Be firm and clear in expectations as well as consequences should the change not occur.

background information. Chapter 3 explores the roles and responsibilities of a successful manager as change leader. Chapter 4 discusses skills and competencies of a change leader. Chapter 5 contains tools for self-diagnosis, along with personal development and action-planning activities. In chapter 6 are tools of the trade, including specific tools and resources useful in change leadership. Finally, chapter 7 offers a compilation of helpful resources for managers eager to expand their knowledge and understanding of the subject.

TWO

The Nature of Change

Our dilemma is that we hate change and love it at the same time; what we want is for things to remain the same but get better.

—Sydney Harris

The rate of change is increasing, driven by global and domestic competition, rapidly evolving markets, technological innovations, changing workforce demographics, mergers and acquisitions, government regulation, and societal scrutiny of business practices. In response, most organizations engage in moderate change initiatives at least once a year and major changes every four or five.[1] Not that these changes are necessarily successful. The statistics on change given in Chapter 1 paint a different picture.

Still, organizational leaders dive head first and often with a great deal of enthusiasm in pursuit of change, oblivious to or in denial of the harsh realities they are about to face. Why the blissful ignorance? Much of this attitude is rooted in common myths and assumptions of change.

MYTHS AND REALITIES OF CHANGE

Assumptions regarding change are as varied and unique as the individuals and organizations that hold them. Unfortunately, mistaken beliefs result in the application of faulty strategies and plans that can cause a huge drain on an organization's ability to deal with change. Some of the most commonly held misbeliefs are as follows: (1) organizations are rationally functioning systems that adjust strategically to changing conditions, (2) employees operate in the best interests of the organization, (3) individuals engage in change because of its merits, (4) change can occur without creating conflict in the system, (5) successful long-term change can be accomplished through short-term leadership, (6) change is easy, (7) change is always good, (8) conflict is always bad, (9) leadership/management always wants change, while only employees resist change, (10) people must be forced to accept change, and (11) people opt to be architects of the change affecting them (see Table 2.1).

These unrealistic beliefs increase expectations among organizations and their members that simply cannot be achieved. Ultimately, faulty assumptions are demotivating, resulting in long-term negative impacts on morale and performance. Consequently, employees are not driven to adopt change.

NATURE OF CHANGE

Understanding the concept of change helps managers function as leaders of change. One of the first steps in developing an understanding of change involves examining types of change. Common changes at the corporate level are strategic, structural, and cultural, typically involving incorporation of new technologies, different leadership, mergers, downsizing, and expansion.

Change may be viewed from an evolutionary perspective as *transitional, transformational,* or *developmental* (see Table 2.2). Transitional change is the most common and basic, simply enhancing the current state via reorganization or reengineering, changing structure or procedures, utilizing new technology, or deciding to expand. Changes such as these may be department or division specific, or organization-wide, and are orchestrated by management. Transformational change represents a radical, fundamental shift from the current state, involving personal behaviors and mind-set. Changing the culture; setting new, drastically different strategy; or being acquired by a dominant firm and being forced to conform to its ways are examples of transformational change. Developmental change flows from

Table 2.1
Myths and Realites of Change

Myth of Change	Reality of Change
Organizations are rationally functioning systems that adjust strategically to changing conditions.	Organizations operate irrationally (because they're composed of people) and are wired to protect the status quo.
Employees operate in the best interests of the organization.	People act in their own best interests, often seeking to preserve or enhance number one. Further, they only want to know what's in it for them.
Individuals engage in change because of its merits.	Most people engage in change to avoid unnecessary difficulties or personal pain.
Change can occur without creating conflict in the system.	By definition, change upsets the current state and will always create some degree of conflict. Effective change management understands, allows, and prepares for conflict. Institutions are often unrealistic about the amount of conflict that occurs as a result of change, and naively expect change to be accepted wholeheartedly by employees.
Successful long-term change can be accomplished through short-term leadership.	Short-term leadership typically lacks the commitment and long-term foresight necessary to make change last – in essence, they don't have to live with the consequences of their decisions.
Change is easy.	Rarely. In fact, effective change processes are quite complex, as are the individuals required to embrace change.
Change is always good.	Not always. Change is often ill-conceived or poorly planned. Further, most institutions do not refer to their guiding principles and values when initiating change, but rather are reacting to external pressures such as changing regulations or the need for greater revenue.
Conflict is always bad.	Not always. A certain amount of conflict can be healthy, particularly when it acts as a catalyst for positive change.
Leadership / management always wants change while only employees resist.	Quite the contrary. Leaders have their own preferences and agendas, which don't always align with the proposed change.

(continued)

**Table 2.1
(continued)**

People must be forced to accept change.	Although many fear change, the fault usually lies with management's failure to properly communicate the reasons for and benefits of change. Well-planned and communicated change may have advocates at all levels within the firm.
People opt to be architects of the change affecting them.	Most individuals do not participate in a pro-active manner in initiating change, preferring instead to be its victims.

an overall organizational philosophy of continuous growth and development that taps the synergy of valued, high-performing employees engaged in meaningful work. Developmental organizations continually scan their internal and external environments for opportunities, making regular, incremental changes. They provide motivating, healthy work environments that encourage innovation, personal renewal, involvement, partnering, and a sense of ownership among organizational members. Developmental firms build competitive advantage through people by maximizing their talents and avoiding radical changes so indicative of poor planning and management.

Additionally, change is often defined as *micro* or *macro* in scope:

- Micro changes are small, manageable, and common transitions, such as adopting a new departmental procedure, adding a new staff member, or participating in training and development programs. Also called "first-order change," this type deals with daily routines, activities, problems, issues, and circumstances. First-order changes occur naturally as the institution grows and develops, representing continuous, minor improvements to the system.
- Institutional changes are large-scale transitions that affect interactions, reporting relationships, and responsibilities. Examples include downsizing, reorganization, and acquisition. Institution-wide changes are also called "second-order change" and represent a fundamental shift in the firm. This is transformational change, whereby leaders question their basic assumptions upon examination of the organization's culture, core processes (e.g., structure, management, decision making, performance management system), vision, mission, values, goals, and strategies. Second-order changes are thoroughly integrated into the organization and transform its basic nature.

Table 2.2
Types of Change

Type Of Change	Driver	Examples
Management	Transitional "Enhances what is"	New technology, policies, or procedures. Reorganization. Structural change. Expansion. Downsizing.
Leadership	Transformational "Fundamental shift in mind-set and behaviors"	Cultural change. Radically new strategy. Acquisition by another firm.
Organizational Philosophy	Developmental "Improved conditions and performance; synergy"	Continually assessing internal and external environments and making incremental shifts. Providing meaningful work. Creating work environments conducive to motivation, growth, and development. Rewarding innovation.

- Macro changes are massive transitions that alter one's life or change one's assumptions, values, or beliefs. The attack on Pearl Harbor in 1941 and the events of September 11, 2001, are prime examples, convincing most Americans that distance doesn't mean safety, and terrorism is a very real threat.

Micro change occurs when "I" change; institutional change is when "we" change; macro change involves "everyone." Although the term *macro* sounds all-encompassing, it seldom occurs. When it does, however, it dramatically affects our lives. Such change alters the way we think and behave forever.

Managers as organizational champions of change will face micro changes on a daily basis—these changes are sometimes quite subtle. Institutional changes occur less frequently, impact a greater audience, and will, therefore, test the manager's abilities on a broader scale. Macro changes are more societal in nature, and thus beyond the typical manager's scope of organizational responsibility. They do, however, influence an individual's thoughts and behavior, which eventually translate to organizational settings.

REACTIONS TO CHANGE

We are all, at times, resistors as well as instigators of change.

—Paul R. Lawrence

People approach and experience change in different ways; it is very personal. When faced with change, individuals may exhibit a range of responses such as fear, acceptance, skepticism, denial, resistance, and so forth. Next we explore individual reactions to change, including confusion or understanding, adoption of innovation, and the four phases of response.

Confusion or Understanding

When individuals comprehend the possibility of an impending change, two possible outcomes exist: *confusion* or *understanding*.[2] Confusion reduces the probability of adequate preparation and favorable reception of change, whereas understanding advances the transformation process to the acceptance phase. Awareness does not necessarily mean that one has a complete understanding of the impact of change. For example, an individual may know that a change is imminent but may be unclear about the nature, depth, breadth, basic rationale, or expected impact of the change.

Understanding the nature and intent of change is the first step in acceptance. Those who are aware of and comprehend a change can encourage and facilitate it. The possible outcomes for the understanding stage are as follows:

- *Negative perception*—employees who have a negative perception toward the institutional change decrease their support for change and may demonstrate resistant behaviors and actions.
- *Positive perception*—employees with a positive perception of change increase their support, which enhances the likelihood of change acceptance.

Once people perceive a change as positive, they must decide whether they are going to support it. A positive perception of change and the actions required to make change happen are quite different efforts. For example, individuals may not have the energy to implement change, regardless of their perception of it. When employees perceive a change as positive, however, they are better prepared to support the effort.

Adoption of Innovations

Everett Rogers explains the process of change in his research into adoption of innovations (changes).[3] An innovation is any idea, practice, procedure, or object perceived as new by an individual—in essence, some sort of change. The degree of newness for the individual determines his or her reaction to the change. Adoption of the new idea or practice is influenced by how the change is communicated over time via certain channels among members of a system.

Stages of adoption include *awareness* of the innovation, *interest* in the change, *trial,* the *decision* to continue or quit, and *adoption* of the innovation into one's lifestyle. Five types of individuals are categorized on the basis of their general acceptance of change as *innovators* (2.5% of the population), *early adopters* (13.5%), *early majority* (34%), *late majority* (34%), and *laggards* (16%) (see Figure 2.1). Innovators thrive on change, are venturesome information seekers, and are among the first to embrace a change and take pride in doing so. Early adopters are supportive of change and willing to take on new challenges. They are opinion leaders and trendsetters who are generally respected, influential members of the organization. The early majority are deliberate accepters of change after observing its impact on innovators and the early adopters; they may be initially uncomfortable but are solid performers who eventually accept the change. The late majority are skeptical and occasionally succumb to peer pressure in order to change; and laggards are traditional, steadfast individuals who often attempt to hold on to the past by resisting change or completely rejecting it.

Certain personality variables have been associated with earlier versus later adopters of change. In general, compared to later adopters, earlier adopters

- have a more favorable attitude toward change
- are better able to cope with uncertainty and risk
- have a greater ability to deal with abstractions
- are less dogmatic than later adopters
- are more rational
- are less fatalistic
- have higher aspirations (for formal education, occupations, and so forth)
- have more change agent contact
- have greater exposure to interpersonal communication channels
- are more knowledgeable of innovations
- have a higher degree of opinion leadership[4]

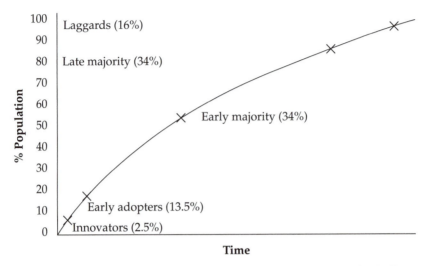

Figure 2.1 Adoption of Innovations adapted from discussion by E. Rogers, *Diffusion of Innovations*, 4th edition, 1995.

Clearly, members of the late majority and laggards, representing half of the population, are most resistant to change. Managers must understand that, given even the most favorable circumstances and well-planned change, nearly half of all employees simply have a predisposition against change. Members of the late majority and laggards will require a great deal of persuasion, if this is at all possible.

Four Phases of Response to Change

Managers as change leaders may find research by Cynthia Scott and Dennis Jaffe, combined with Larry Senn, tremendously useful. Scott and Jaffe identified four phases of response to change: denial, resistance, exploration, and commitment.[5] Senn's "emotional cycle of change" includes five phases: uninformed optimism, informed pessimism, giving up, informed optimism, and rewarding completion.[6] A combination of both perspectives is illustrated in Figure 2.2. Each phase represents the manifestation of specific behaviors and emotions of those facing change.

Denial results from insufficient knowledge related to the impending change, and occurs when individuals believe that the change will have little, if any, impact on them personally. This honeymoon feeling is based on positive, often naïve or *uninformed optimism* due to lack of information or data about the change initiative. Denial can be overcome by involving individuals in the change process, providing information via appropriate communications, soliciting feedback from individuals regarding their perceptions of and feelings toward change, and helping them understand their role in change and how it will impact them personally.

The second phase, *resistance,* occurs when the transformation becomes personal. Individuals begin to doubt the appropriateness of the change as a result of receiving additional information—accurate or not—regarding the change. In this phase, *informed pessimism* occurs when people realize the inconvenience, difficulty, or hardship they will personally face, and some begin to actively resist. Managing resistance starts with engaging resisters in dialogue (two-way communication) that reveals the underlying reasons for their stance (e.g., poor communication, perceived unrealistic goals, fear of loss of status, concerns regarding the viability of the change, etc.). Understanding the cause(s) of resistance enables change agents to address concerns, take corrective action, earn employee trust, and engender support.

The critical point in the change initiative—*giving up*—is reached when extremely disappointed, frustrated, or angry employees disengage emotionally or physically from the change effort. Some leave the organization entirely because they have serious reservations or a low tolerance for change. At this point, we must engage employees or let them go.

Exploration, the third phase, reflects progress in the journey toward acceptance of the change initiative. In this phase, people accept the reality of change and seek positive outcomes. Although cynicism does not suddenly disappear, it lessens as employees understand the eventuality of or necessity for change. *Informed optimism* surfaces as more and more concerns are resolved; individuals become increasingly confident and move toward the next stage. In this phase, continued communication and celebrations of small victories encourage individuals to explore further and move closer to commitment.

The fourth phase is characterized by acceptance of change as a positive opportunity. Employees demonstrate their *commitment* to the change by supporting and managing its implementation. In this stage, employees perceive *rewarding completion* as they integrate new actions or behaviors in their daily work. Celebration and rewards are critical at this point to encourage individuals to solidify change in the fabric of their work and the culture of the organization.

Implications for Managers

Some individuals navigate quickly through the change process; others need more time, stall, or vacillate between phases. One's predisposition toward change, combined with factors such as organizational culture, trust, and flow of information, among others, determines one's location

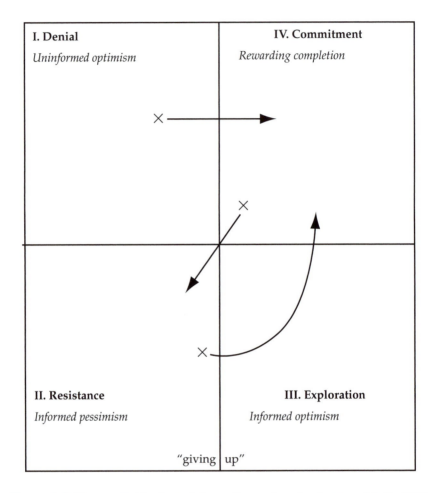

Figure 2.2 Change Grid adapted from discussions by Scott and Jaffe 1988 and Senn 1989.

on the change grid. Additionally, both internal and external factors may drive our progress toward, or away from, change. Family issues, loss of resources, or unexpected events such as 9/11 may compel even someone in the commitment phase to reconsider his or her acceptance of a change.

Understanding human reactions to change, responding appropriately, communicating, and involving people are the keys to leading employees through the change process and to acceptance. Providing data, answering questions, selling the benefits of change, and involving employees in planning and implementing change help people overcome resistance and work through change. Individuals desire information, input, and opportunities to succeed. By valuing individuals' contributions and respecting the energy of dissent, leaders of change can promote effective change efforts in a dynamic environment.

RESISTANCE TO CHANGE

It is important to understand that individuals at all organizational levels resist change—from the front line to the executive offices. Why? Resistance is a natural part of the change process as individuals and organizations struggle to maintain a sense of equilibrium. Further, we each approach and react to change differently—rational or not. Resistance to change is rooted in our innate personalities, experiences, biases, expectations, and predisposition toward change. And when individuals resist change, so too does the organization. Leaders of change understand this intensely personal side of change and, therefore, proactively learn as much as possible about those who will be involved in the change efforts. Understanding individual behavior leads to understanding organizational behavior, and ultimately to successfully navigating through change.

Individual Resistance to Change

People are inherently resistant to change; thus avoiding or resisting change is human nature. As a result, organizations are resistant to change, preferring to preserve the status quo. Although resisting change is natural, failing to change can be deadly. Leaders, managers, and employees who fail to change may find themselves without jobs. Businesses that don't change, for example, eventually disappear, falling victim to acquisition or a slow (or fast), natural death. Following are some common reasons why individuals resist change:

- fear of the unknown
- fear of failure
- fear of loss of security
- perceived loss of status, control, or power
- uncertainty
- low tolerance for change
- risk aversion
- threatened self-interests/desire not to lose something of value
- change may add work to already overburdened employees
- no incentive to change
- disruption of routine

- peer pressure
- misunderstanding of change and its implications
- belief that the change doesn't make sense
- lack of input into the change
- previously penalized during/after change efforts (or for failure to effectively change)
- organizational culture doesn't support change
- poor organizational structure
- limited resources to support change
- ineffective performance management system
- lack of trust of management
- manager's initial reaction to change or initial resistance may set the stage for employee resistance
- lack of effective guidance (managerial)
- people in power are driven to maintain the status quo, not dramatically change it
- lack of clarity about the desired change—who, what, why, and when
- belief that they are being dictated to

Understanding an individual's personal resistance to change enables the manager to then address the employee's concerns and overcome the hesitance. We discuss overcoming resistance to change later in this chapter.

Recent research has identified five common factors when people and change are involved in organizational settings: (1) loss of status and former sphere of influence, (2) lack of understanding of the firm's intentions, (3) fierce fight for survival, (4) increased workloads (e.g., due to downsizing, employees leaving voluntarily or involuntarily), and (5) the spillover effect on personal lives.[7] Clearly, individual and organizational responses to change are intertwined. Next, we explore symptoms of resistance to change.

Symptoms of Resistance

Resistance to change is as unique and multifaceted as the person being asked to change. Words and behaviors manifest themselves as resistance in various ways (see Table 2.3).

It is important to identify and address the *cause* of the symptoms of resistance. Underlying causes fuel resistance; when these causes are understood, they can be managed. Attempting to deal with symptoms (rather than causes) yields shortsighted and often unsuccessful efforts to implement change.

Table 2.3
Indicators of Resistance to Change

Words	Behaviors
It doesn't/won't affect me.	Withdrawal.
Been there, done that, and it didn't work.	Aggression, arguing, acting out.
	Blaming, gossip.
This is another management fad.	Overuse of humor.
Just wait, this will pass.	Refusal to attempt change.
They'll forget about it.	Negativism, refusal to attempt change.
That's a stupid idea.	Resistance, sabotage of the change ef-
They can't make me change.	fort, increased absenteeism.
It won't work.	Slowdown of work, resistance, sabo-
I like the way we did it before.	tage.
Why should I? (What's in it for me?)	Slowdown of work, resistance, refusal.

Organizational Resistance to Change: The Immune System

Individual and organizational behaviors and reactions are remarkably similar. Organizations are, after all, merely collections of people making decisions necessary to achieve common organizational goals. Thus, individual behaviors manifest themselves as organizational actions—the two cannot be separated.

Organizations, like the human body, are systems composed of many subsystems that must function efficiently and in concert.[8] Organizations are complex networks of interrelated people and processes working together across multiple layers and departments while engaging in diverse functions. The most functional and healthiest systems are dynamic and responsive, capable of recognizing and responding to change in a positive manner. Why, then, is change so difficult for individuals and organizations? Why are we so resistant? The answer lies within the innate responses of the body to change—responses regulated by the immune system.

The immune system is a complex yet elegant network designed to protect the body. The immune system's protective ability is remarkable: it can detect and respond to minor intrusions such as a sliver; it can identify and destroy infectious agents such as bacteria and viruses, and it is able to recognize cancer cells, which are the body's own cells growing out of control.[9] The body is protected as the immune system identifies and subsequently removes or isolates the threat or foreign entity. The body's highly critical immune system occasionally overreacts to a threat or perceives a "self" cell to be a foreign entity, with disastrous results (serious disease, even death). Within organizations, this similar response occurs when individuals overreact to impending change.

Failure of the immune system or misjudgment of a threat may yield catastrophic results. Infection, illness, and occasionally death occur when invaders such as bacteria or viruses escape detection. Similarly, organizations are sometimes blind to impending threats posed by competitors, the economy, or changing customer wants.

At times, the immune system works too well. Organ implants and healthy tissue grafts fail when the body determines that they are nonself and proceeds to attack them.[10] Within organizations we see similar derailment of potentially positive, healthy changes by individuals or groups threatened by the new initiative.

Sentinels of the Immune System

One key mediator of the body's immune response is the macrophage: a large, rather slow cell that moves throughout the body in search of invading or foreign entities such as bacteria, viruses, cancer cells, or nonbiological materials (e.g., slivers or surgical implants). Macrophages are the *sentinels of the immune system,* residing at every portal of entry to the body—the eyes, nose, mucosa, lungs, gastrointestinal tract, and so forth.[11]

Upon encountering a foreign entity, the macrophage may engulf and subsequently destroy it, or attach to it. If the foreign entity is too large for the macrophage or several to digest, they begin to physically separate the intruder from the rest of the body. This "foreign body response" protects us by isolating and destroying bacteria, viruses, cancer cells, and more.[12] However, it is also responsible for rejection of desirable implants and tissue grafts. Regardless of the source or purpose of intrusion, the immune system is diligent and unbiased in its survival-mode response—similar to the rejection of new ideas in an organizational setting. Often an individual's response (like that of the cell) is a defensive move that lacks consideration of the overall well-being of the system. In many instances, both the body and the organization would benefit if a change was allowed.

Individual and Organizational Responses to Change

The human body responds quickly to intrusions, which trigger a response that is local, systemic, or both.[13] A *local* response is characterized by inflammation (swelling), coagulation (clotting), infection, or tumorigenesis (production of tumors).[14] Local responses such as infection and coagulation can be prevented or treated if detected early.

Systemic, or whole body, responses such as hypersensitivity, embolization (typically blockage of a vessel), toxemia, or metastasis (a system out of control, as when cancer is rapidly spreading) may be the result of a

Table 2.4
Local, Systemic, and Organizational Responses to Change

Local Responses	Systemic Responses	Organizational Equivalents/ Responses
Inflammation redness, swelling, pain	Hypersensitivity unusual, excessive, or uncontrolled reactions	Fear, denial, overreaction
Coagulation clotting	Embolization clot forms, lodges, breaks free, then clogs	Resistance, steadfast refusal
Infection contamination, disease	Toxemia poison	Rumors, sabotage, para- lyzing fear
Tumorigenesis production of tumors, especially malignancies	Metastasis out of control	Chaos

Source: Gilley, Godek, and Gilley, *The Organizational Immune System*, 2005.

major attack on the body or of a minor intrusion left untreated.[15] Systemic responses are often beyond control and require drastic measures to curb (see Table 2.4).

Similarities between the Human Body and Organizations

Human and organizational systems are remarkably similar—both are complex yet delicate collections of interrelated functions. Organizations are simply collections of people—they are firms run by people for people.

A comparison can be made between the immune system's macrophages and people in organizations. Macrophages are gatekeepers, positioned at every portal of entry to the system, ready to attack any invaders of the body. Some are specific, others more general in their vigilant defense. Organizations, similarly, have their own gatekeepers, skeptics, and defenders ready to protect the status quo. Just as macrophages engulf (ingest) objects and present them to other components of the immune system for further interrogation, people encounter new ideas and form opinions, which they then present to other employees for acceptance or rejection. In a cellular setting the body responds based on the initial interrogation by the macrophage, in which a threat may be real or simply perceived. Similarly, employees may view organizational change as a real threat, even when the change is potentially positive (see Table 2.5).

Clearly, resistance to change is an innate response intended to protect us from threats. Individuals and their organizations are wired to preserve

Table 2.5
Similarities between the Human Body and Organizational
Responses to Change

Body's Response to Intrusion	Organization's Response to Change
Intruding material attracts proteins	Organizational leaders explore the possibility of change
Cells sample the material	Employees ask questions, seek information
Cells fuse to form giant cells and secrete protein signaling agents to recruit additional macrophages and a second cell type, fibroblasts	Rumors, gossip; Initial fear and resistance take hold; intrusion is isolated, resources cut off Employees form alliances against the change, become vocal, and call in reinforcements
Fibroblasts begin to synthesize collagen	Alliances build, resistance solidifies
The intruding material is surrounded (which manifests itself as inflammation)	Avoidance, rejection, sabotage; The change is insulated, alienated from the organization, ultimately rejected

the status quo and maintain balance, occasionally overreacting by perceiving even desirable change as a negative. The challenge lies in overcoming this inherent response and allowing individuals to see the positive aspects of change.

OVERCOMING RESISTANCE TO CHANGE

How do we help individuals and organizations lessen resistance and embrace change? A concept as complex as change cannot be addressed with a simple, quick fix or a one-size-fits-all strategy. Although human and organizational reactions can be predicted with some degree of accuracy, they cannot be guaranteed.

Change is very personal; one's approach to change is a unique combination of personality (e.g., prone to acceptance), values, culture, and more. Resistance to change, although natural, can be lessened. Reducing resistance to change involves mitigating or removing the barriers to change (see chapter 1). Given that these barriers include components of the organizational system itself (e.g., poor leadership, dysfunctional culture, lack of management support, and so forth), it is important to remember that strategies for overcoming resistance must focus on all levels of the organization, from executive to the front line. Communication, training, involvement, stress management, negotiation, and coercion are commonly employed strategies.[16] Also included is management/leadership training and development, due to the belief that management typically drives change and, thus, should be skilled in change implementation and overcoming resistance.

- *Management/leadership training and development*—all supervisors, managers, directors, and executives must be skilled in planning, implementing, and monitoring change; understanding the range of human reactions to change; communicating effectively; reducing resistance; and gaining commitment. Enhancing management skills and talents in these areas is essential and should be an ongoing priority within organizations, given the constant nature of change.
- *Communication*—open, honest two-way communication reduces resistance by keeping all stakeholders informed about the change. Frequent, effective communication reduces fear of the unknown and promotes the positive aspects of the change. Feedback from those involved in change (or about to be) may provide valuable information regarding the change and its impact, processes, and long-term viability.
- *Education and training*—individuals at all levels of the firm benefit from training specific to the change. Education and training reduce stress while increasing one's confidence with a change and reducing fear of the unknown. It is important to allow individuals ample time and a safe environment in which to practice new procedures or incorporate new ways of work into their daily routines.
- *Involvement*—individuals support what they create; involvement creates psychological ownership of decisions and accountability for their success. Involvement helps people understand their role and how the change will affect them personally.
- *Understand causes of resistance and take corrective action*—resistance may be justified when its cause is rooted in some flaw inherent to the change or the organization itself. Resistance may be a perfectly natural reaction to an ill-conceived or implemented change, dysfunctional culture or processes, poor leadership or management, or lack of sufficient resources to implement the change. Flaws such as these must be corrected or the change will fail to yield desired results.
- *Stress management*—formal and informal stress management programs and techniques help individuals cope with change. Formal stress management may include employee assistance programs or on-

site counselors; informal programs often encourage individual stress reduction methods such as meditation, breathing, or other relaxation techniques.

- *Negotiation and coercion*—may be necessary when individuals may lose as a result of the change. Negotiation offers benefits that may offset potential losses and allows people to become part of the process. Coercion may be necessary when time is of the essence and other tactics have proven unsuccessful. Coercion, however, fails to generate commitment for change, often erodes trust, and may lead to increased turnover.
- *Celebration and rewards*—help anchor the change into the system. Rewarding individual and group efforts at change sends a powerful message—that the change is meaningful and those who have struggled to incorporate it are valuable. Celebrating milestones provides a measure of progress, enables individuals to blow off steam, and helps paint the change as a positive experience.

Resistance must be understood and managed on a personal level. Leaders of change take it upon themselves to understand individual and organizational responses (resistance) to change, prepare for the inevitable resistance to change to surface, address each individual's specific reasons for resisting the change, and involve employees in the change process and seek their input.

CHANGE MANAGEMENT

Successful change results from strategic planning, thorough communication, fierce dedication, teamwork, and a keen understanding of human nature (particularly motivation and resistance). Change-management models attempt to guide organizations and their managers through change.

Early change models followed a three-step process that involved diagnosing and preparing an organization for change, engaging in change, and anchoring new ways into the culture.[17] Lewin's classic model of change, for example, consists of *unfreezing, movement,* and *refreezing. Unfreezing* refers to conditioning individuals and organizations for change, examining individuals' readiness for change, and establishing ownership. Momentum builds when stakeholders align to introduce change and plan its implementation. *Movement,* also called "transformation," occurs when individuals engage in change initiatives. In the final phase, *refreezing,* individuals incorporate the change into their daily routine and reestablish equilibrium personally or within the firm. New behaviors are

Table 2.6
Change Models

Step	Lewin's Model	Gilley's 7-step Model	Ulrich's 7-step Model	Kotter's 8-step Model
1	Unfreeze	Communicate the Urgency for Change	Lead Change	Establish a Sense of Urgency
2	Movement	Provide Leadership	Create a Shared Need	Form a Powerful Guiding Coalition
3	Refreeze	Create Ownership and Support	Shape a Vision	Create a Vision
4		Create a Shared Vision	Mobilize Commitment	Communicate the Vision
5		Implement and Manage Change	Change Systems and Structures	Empower Others to Act on the Vision
6		Integrate Change into the Culture	Monitor Progress	Plan for and Create Short-term Wins
7		Measure and Monitor Change	Make Change Last	Consolidate Improvements and Produce Still More Change
8				Institutionalize New Approaches

Sources: Gilley and Gilley 2003; Kotter 1996; Lewin 1951; Ulrich 1998.

solidified and ultimately deemed the norm. Continually reminding affected parties of the purposes and benefits of change helps solidify the change.

Building on the early models, researchers have developed more extensive, multistep frameworks that incorporate leadership, employee involvement and commitment, monitoring, rewards, and more. Table 2.6 compares some of the popular models.

Although these models provide valuable guidelines for planning and managing change, they assume that the effort will be successful provided all steps are followed in sequence. These models fail to recognize the complexity of change, nor do they suggest appropriate action when change efforts are sidelined. Therefore, a more comprehensive, realistic set of steps for successful change implementation follows in Table 2.7.

Understanding individual responses to change enables organizations to prepare for change more effectively, create a culture of change, and help employees through the difficult process.

Table 2.7
Comprehensive Model for Change

UNFREEZE	1. understand that change is immensely complex linear
	2. understand individual and organizational responses (resistance) to change, and how to deal with these responses
	3. create a culture that supports change
	4. establish a vision for change
	5. build a guiding coalition for the change
	6. sell the change to individuals at all levels of the organization; help people understand that the change is necessary, urgent; teach that change is good, desirable
	7. remove barriers to action
CHANGE	8. involve employees at all levels of the organization in the change process (including initial decision making, planning, implementation, monitoring, and rewarding)
	9. communicate proficiently; solicit input and share information with those impacted by the change; lack of information breeds fear
	10. prepare for and plan responses to resistance; treat resistance to change as an opportunity; understand that resistance is a symptom of a deeper problem (e.g., poor management or strategy, ineffective communication, etc.)
	11. deal with employees and their reactions individually, not as a group
	12. execute the change in small increments
	13. constantly monitor progress of the change initiative and refine/adjust as needed
REFREEZE	14. reward individuals and groups for engaging in change
	15. celebrate short- and long-term wins
	16. solidify the change in the newly emerged culture

CONDITIONS NECESSARY FOR CHANGE

Change doesn't occur in a vacuum. Managers make change happen and last when they set up conditions that support the change effort and nourish those involved. People change when they have the capacity—the ability and the willingness—to do so.[18] *Ability* involves possessing the necessary skills and knowing how to use them. *Willingness* implies motivation to apply one's skills and knowledge. When one lacks either ability or willingness, successful adaptation to change is unlikely. Skill or knowledge deficiencies may be addressed with education, training, or informal mentoring. Resistant behavior stems from a lack of motivation and may be addressed through dialogue, performance management, communication, and individual coaching.

Change initiatives bring about desired results when enlightened leadership successfully introduces and sustains change. Managers and all those involved must have highly visible commitment to change maintained throughout all phases, from diagnosis through implementation and evaluation.

Effective change efforts are intertwined with multiple parts of the organization, directed by managers acting as champions of change, based on an effective diagnosis of the firm, and consistent with business conditions. Employees must clearly see the relationship between the change effort and the organization's mission, goals, and guiding principles. Finally, individuals and organizations must be at an optimal point of readiness for change in order for it to occur. When these conditions are present, managers are more successful in championing desired change initiatives.

RULES OF CHANGE

At best, change is challenging. It is easy to get caught up in the many models, formulas, and schemes offered by well-intended, battle-scarred change masters. At the end of the day, however, a few rules help define the essence of change:

1. Change is not easy, cheap, or fast.
2. Change is personal—people change, not organizations.
3. People need to know what's in it for them before they'll willingly change.
4. People will inherently resist change.
5. Communication is critical.
6. People change at different rates.
7. Change produces conflict—it is inevitable and unavoidable; be prepared!
8. Not all change is good or even necessary.

CONCLUSION

Change has many faces—fear, optimism, confusion, and chaos, to name a few. Understanding the nature of change is the first step in its management. Change leaders understand the myths and realities of change, our innate resistance and responses to situations involving change, and how to establish conditions necessary for successful change to occur.

Roles and Responsibilities of a Change Leader

We must change to master change.

—Lyndon B. Johnson

Everyone is, or can be, a change agent, depending on the situation. At some point, we each engage in the role, just as, to some degree, we each possess the necessary skills. In essence, we are all responsible for change. In a work setting, the ability to manage change effectively may be the most critical skill of modern managers and leaders. One cannot escape the inevitable march of change, so it makes sense to heighten our understanding of and ability to effect change.

Organizations that have faced the reality of change identify and nurture change competencies in their employees, managers, and executives. They hire and promote individuals who possess the knowledge, skills, and attributes necessary to become effective agents of change (see chapter 4, "Skills and Competencies of a Change Leader").

An activity as complex as change requires a great deal of commitment and skill on the part of change leaders. Few of us are born with the innate ability to expertly initiate and execute change, a point underscored by the vast number of disappointing change efforts reported by organizations throughout time.

Effective change champions have taken it upon themselves to acquire the needed knowledge and skills to successfully move their people and organizations forward. They understand the complexity of change and human reactions to it, and hone their skills and toolboxes accordingly to effectively execute needed change.

Management and leadership are different functions, yet successful change implementation requires both. Therefore, making change happen taps both the management *and* the leadership talents of individuals (see also the section "Management versus Leadership" in chapter 1).

Organizational change leaders are sometimes perceived with a combination of admiration and fear—admiration for their abilities to secure results, fear of the impact their proposed changes may have on us. Effective change leaders minimize fear and elevate commitment by engaging their talents in the specific roles of *visionary, inspirer, supporter, problem solver,* and *change manager* (see Table 3.1).

VISIONARY

Leaders hold a unique place in the hearts of followers. We see them as charismatic, larger than life, and capable of almost anything. In spite of their daring and risk taking, they often (but not always) emerge even stronger from their battles. "Leaders must be able to stand before us and confidently express an attractive image of the future—and we must be able to believe that they have the ability to take us there."[1]

Challenge the Status Quo

Leaders look for opportunities and for challenges. In fact, they actively search for ways to change. In doing so, leaders raise the bar in demonstration of their quest for improvement. The status quo represents complacency, mediocrity, and eventual decline—conditions that are unacceptable to most leaders.

Imagine the Future

Leaders have the ability to craft a mental picture of a state that doesn't yet exist. A vision of change portrays a vivid picture of the future. Sometimes a vision represents the ideal or unrealistic perfect world; occasionally it is grounded in the reality of organizational and individual capabilities.

Table 3.1
Roles and Responsibilities of a Change Leader

Role	Responsibilities
Visionary	Challenge the status quo. Imagine the future. Develop a stewardship philosophy. Align the change with organizational vision, mission, strategy, and individual goals. Articulate the vision.
Inspirer	Sell the change. Energize and involve others. Live/model the change.
Supporter	Create a culture of change. Provide resources. Involve others (when the few decide for the many, anger and resistance surface). Encourage creativity and innovation. Communicate, communicate, communicate. Own the change –publicly demonstrate active personal involvement in the change process. Model the behavior, be consistent with organizational values, ensure congruence of messages and behaviors. Enhance own skills. Recognize and reward.
Problem Solver	Analyze the situation. Craft creative solutions. Monitor constantly.
Change Manager	Coordinate change. Communicate. Establish clear goals and expectations – clearly articulate expectations and objectives, be explicit. Involve others. Anticipate and address personnel problems and conflict. Recognize and reward (the right things). Make change last.

Many change efforts fail when leaders neglect to involve employees in development of the change vision. A shared vision built collaboratively by individuals at all levels of the organization taps their collective knowledge, creativity, and strengths, while minimizing the perception that the vision is simply a wild idea by an out-of-touch executive team. People support what they create; therefore, involving them in crafting the change vision improves the chance of success.

A good vision clarifies the direction of change and motivates individuals to take action. An effective vision

- acknowledges that sacrifices will be necessary but makes clear that these sacrifices will yield particular benefits and personal satisfactions that are far superior to those available today—or tomorrow—without attempting to change
- is imaginable in that it conveys a picture of what the future will look like
- is desirable because it appeals to the long-term interests of those who have a stake in the enterprise
- is feasible, enabling organizations to develop realistic, attainable goals
- is focused, providing guidance in making decisions
- is flexible, allowing individual initiative and alternative responses in light of changing conditions, and
- is easy to communicate[2]

Philosophy of Stewardship

True leaders put the welfare of their organizations and their members above their own. Personal gain and glory are not issues. Stewards are change leaders, driven by the desire to help their organizations (and employees) improve. They fight tirelessly to support their people, achieve their vision, and secure success for all involved. Employees, customers, and society benefit when organizations are healthy, productive, creative, and meeting the needs of stakeholders.

Align the Change with Organizational Vision, Mission, Strategy, and Individual Goals

Organizational vision should drive mission, which should drive strategy, which should drive division and individual goals. Thus, appropriate change initiatives support goals, strategy, mission, and vision. Lack of congruence between proposed changes and existing strategy leads people to question the validity of the change, which leads to resistance and, often, disappointing results.

Articulate the Vision

Visionaries are often quite skillful at passionately communicating their vision. Sometimes described as charismatic or compelling, these change leaders paint a picture of the future with colorful words that appeal to our senses and draw us in. They frame messages around an impressive goal with an emotional appeal that captivates the audience. For a rare few this is an innate talent cultivated over time and manifesting itself at an opportune moment. Most of us, however, welcome assistance in crafting the messages necessary to share our ideas. Colleagues, mentors, and communications professionals (writers, editors, speakers) can help us develop and clarify our communications.

INSPIRER

One of the most commonly cited traits of leaders is their ability to inspire others. Change leaders motivate and energize their constituents by meeting their needs—making the change personally beneficial in some meaningful way. Inspiring others entails campaigning for—or selling—the change, involving others, and personally living the change.

Sell the Change

Actively selling change involves identifying specific benefits valuable to each employee while concurrently minimizing potential losses or risks. Any campaign for change begins with an understanding of individuals' needs, hopes, and fears on both personal and professional levels.

Involve Others

Involving employees at all levels of the organization proves powerfully motivating. Joint diagnosis of problems, potential solutions, and opportunities enables individuals to feel ownership of the change along with feeling like worthy contributors to an important effort. Involvement builds alliances that are likely to support the change through thick and thin, long and short term.

Live the Change

Successful leaders live and model the change—they not only talk about the change, they enact it. They are the first to modify their behaviors, practice new ways, and espouse the benefits of change by stepping outside the executive suite and engaging in activities that symbolize the change. Their wholehearted enthusiasm and commitment to the change can be contagious and inspirational in their own right. Conversely, nothing derails a change effort quite like leadership indifference or negativism.

SUPPORTER

Support for change comes in many forms. Servant leaders, for example, enhance the success of change by putting employee needs above their own. Enabling change involves communicating often, providing adequate resources and training (e.g., human, financial, time), anticipating a learning curve, allowing for mistakes, rewarding individual and group change efforts, continually monitoring the process and its progress, making adjustments to the change effort as necessary, and celebrating milestones.

Change efforts exact a heavy emotional toll on people; thus support at all levels and on many fronts proves invaluable.

Create a Culture of Change

Work environments set the stage for success or failure of change. Fear, lack of respect, poor communications, and inadequate resources are among the ingredients of failure. Conversely, supportive work atmospheres encourage a free exchange of ideas and feelings, and provide employees with a safe environment (free from harm or consequences) in which to implement change.

Organizational culture, or "the way we do things around here," reflects the shared beliefs, assumptions, and behaviors acquired over time by members of the firm. Culture evolves gradually, passed on from person to person. At its best, culture provides consistency for employees and protection from sudden shifts (e.g., knee-jerk reactions or adoption of the latest fads) that might threaten its very existence. At its worst, culture may insulate, even suffocate, the organization and its members, preventing actions needed to survive. Dysfunctional culture may inhibit organizations from differentiating between necessary and unnecessary change, and may doom its members to gradual decline.

We are each instruments of our organization's culture; therefore, we have the ability to impact it positively. To create a climate of change, managers should

- plan communications
- demonstrate understanding that change is difficult and very personal
- provide individuals with formal and informal opportunities to give input and feedback
- accept that employees are unique in their approach and reaction to change
- involve impacted individuals in decision making
- recognize and reward those who embrace change

Provide Resources

A common complaint of employees is that they are being asked to do more with less. Change initiatives are no different. Individuals are often challenged to change their work behaviors without benefit of sufficient training, preparation, time, equipment, or other forms of support. Organizations that are dedicated to achieving successful change efforts provide their employees with the tools to change. Managers who are responsible for change actively fight for the resources needed by their employees to implement change successfully.

Partner with and Involve Others

When the few decide for the many, anger and resistance rise. Involving others—treating them like partners—conveys the sense that "we're in this together—*our* success depends on this change." Change leaders understand that individuals support what they help create. Involving people in the change process stresses the importance of their worth as individuals, enhances their self-esteem, taps their wealth of knowledge and experience, builds loyalty (to you), and heightens their commitment to the change.

Encourage Creativity and Innovation

Since change involves engaging in something new, encouraging entrepreneurship, creativity, and innovation proves logical. In the role of supporter, champions of change promote alternative ways of thinking and approaches to opportunities or problems. Brainstorming and individual or group competitions, for example, may yield fun, creative, viable solutions not previously considered. Creativity workshops and rewards for innovations are additional tools.

Communicate, Communicate, Communicate

Communication, or lack thereof, is often cited as one of the most prevalent problems within organizations. Change efforts seem exceptionally subject to poor communications, which exacerbates the problem, particularly when compounded with stress, deadlines, and employee fear. Lack of information breeds fear, paranoia, and resistance to change at all levels. People crave information and want to be in the loop—we want to know "why," "when," "how," and "what's in it for me?" Champions of change plan their communications carefully—from content and timing to appropriate techniques.

In the supporter role, change leaders perfect the art of communication by interacting with employees at all levels and meeting their information and feedback needs. Supporters assess the communication styles of others and adapt their own styles to the situation and audience.

In order of effectiveness, communications are face-to-face, by phone, or in writing (e.g., letters, memos, e-mails). People who process information visually take advantage of face-to-face communications to assess body language; they also like presentations with graphics and written communiqués that they can read, reread, and save for later reference. Those who process information verbally prefer to hear the message one-on-one, in group meetings, or by phone, which allows them to evaluate delivery and speaker tone along with content.

A multifaceted approach that begins with and heavily utilizes one-on-one communications yet incorporates all forms of exchange yields the best results. Face-to-face interactions can be effectively supplemented with written forms that clarify information and provide documentation. Letters, memoranda, and e-mails should not constitute the primary form of data sharing—they're too impersonal and subject to misinterpretation. Personal is best.

Own the Change

Support involves publicly demonstrating active personal involvement in the change process. Wholehearted commitment on the part of change leaders sends a powerful message to followers—that the change is significant and worthwhile. Ownership also implies responsibility; that is, the change represents a personal goal and responsibility of the leader. He or she will be held accountable. As a result, the leader is intensely motivated to help the change succeed.

Model the Behavior

Champions of change model the behaviors they seek to inspire in others. These must be consistent with organizational values to ensure congruence of messages and behaviors with desired change. Sacrifice, for example, is a common theme among those being forced to change, and they want to witness the same from their leaders. Change efforts often require people to take risks while giving up security, routine, and comfort. Change leaders in the supporter role recognize and appreciate the forfeitures made by all involved in the change effort. They willingly make sacrifices for the greater good and the change effort.

Enhance Own Skills

Continuous organizational improvement requires enhancement of individual change skills at all levels—from the front line to the executive offices. Effective leaders model personal and professional development by continually honing their own skills—both formally and informally. Formally, skills may be enhanced by pursuing advanced degrees whose curriculums address change, attending workshops on change, or through coaching. Informally, one's skills improve with practice, through working with others, and by soliciting feedback. Effective leaders promote skills improvement on the part of all employees throughout the firm.

Recognize and Reward

Leaders as supporters of change encourage and reward behaviors that are different from those who are in the role of change manager. The most commonly cited behaviors desired by leaders are loyalty, candor, innovation, risk taking, entrepreneurship, and results. These are rewarded with promotions, opportunity, responsibility, exposure, and positions of influence (leadership or management), among others.

PROBLEM SOLVER

Any effort at change offers opportunities for difficulties to arise—whether organizational, technical, or interpersonal. As most managers will attest, they put out fires every day. As a result, they regularly engage in the role of problem solver—analyzing the situation, crafting and implementing solutions, and monitoring progress.

Analyze the Situation

Effective assessment of the current state begins with SWOT (strengths, weaknesses, opportunities, threats) analysis of affected individuals, units, divisions, or the entire organization. Scanning of the internal environment reveals strengths and weaknesses over which we have control. Examples include leadership talent, human resource capability, resource availability, culture, and effectiveness of policies and procedures. The external environment poses opportunities and threats often beyond our scope of influence, such as increasing competition, restrictive legislation, changing social expectations, and so forth. Only a thorough understanding of a firm's internal and external environments enables informed problem solving. Absent detailed analysis, potential solutions to a firm's problems are based on insufficient data. The result? Disappointing change efforts. SWOT analysis provides change leaders with the information necessary to maximize strengths and opportunities while minimizing weaknesses and threats related to the desired change.

Problem solvers also identify and assess their organization's immune system—that is, their propensity to reject change. To do so,

- Examine the history of response to change in your firm.
- Identify the sentinels (resisters of change) of your immune system.

  What type of change do they hinder?
  How do they inhibit change, specifically?
  Why do they prevent change?

- Deal with these individuals—involve or reassign.

Craft Creative Solutions

Thinking outside the box comes naturally for some, with great difficulty for others. Successful change, however, is the result of seeking new ways to approach old issues. Quite often, management is part of the problem—having developed, supported, and/or enforced current undesirable, ineffective, even dysfunctional practices. Those who have history with the firm may encounter skepticism regarding their abilities or intentions while attempting to implement change.

Creativity is a function of people, enthusiasm, freedom, and support. Collaborating with people who are enthusiastic about the potential change, providing them the freedom to explore and be unconventional without reprisal, and supporting (via public commitment, financial backing, and so forth) new ways of doing business lay the foundation for generating creative solutions.

Constantly Monitor

Staying on top of problems, or one step ahead, requires constant assessment of conditions surrounding the change initiative. Change leaders rely on their own investigation as well as their network of connected organizational members for data, insights, and feedback regarding the state of the environment surrounding the change. Where change is involved, effective evaluation requires personal contact, not impersonal production reports. Dialogue and feedback between and among individuals and groups reveal the true dimensions of change efforts. Regular assessment allows for timely modifications or interventions and potentially prevents or lessens future derailments.

CHANGE MANAGER

Change management, by virtue of its complex nature, must be carefully monitored, lest the initiative get out of control. Successful leaders of change, if not expert at the highly detailed task of coordinating change, surround themselves with those who are. Effectively managing change involves coordinating the entire process, communicating thoroughly and appropriately, establishing clear expectations, engaging those impacted by the change, preparing for personnel issues, rewarding change efforts, and solidifying new ways into the daily operations of the firm.

Coordinate Change

The traditional definition of management is *planning, directing, organizing, and controlling*. The planning function involves systematically making decisions about the goals and activities that an individual, a group, a work unit, or the organization will pursue. Planning activities include analyzing, forecasting, setting objectives, allocating resources, crafting strategies, and determining activities in which the organization will engage to achieve its goals. Above all, change managers balance change with organizational capabilities.

Plans may be short term (less than one year), of intermediate duration (one to five years), or long term (greater than five years). These plans may be developed for individuals, work units, or the entire organization, and may be very general (e.g., improve profitability over the next year) or specific (reduce defects by 10% in the next quarter).

Effectively instituting change requires managers to provide clear direction by determining and communicating specific actionable plans to meet goals and objectives. This is not dictating. Successful directing involves performance coaching, delegation of responsibility, and candid communication with individuals and groups.

The organizing function is assembling and coordinating the resources (human, financial, physical, informational, and other) and activities needed to achieve change goals. Organizing includes specifying job responsibilities, scheduling work assignments, grouping jobs into work units, and creating conditions for people to achieve success.

The controlling function ensures that goals are met. Controlling monitors progress and implements change by comparing actual outcomes to goals. Controlling involves setting performance standards and expectations, monitoring individual and unit progress toward change goals by collecting performance data, providing employees with feedback regarding their performance, and taking action to correct problems or maximize opportunities. Budgeting, information systems, performance appraisals, and disciplinary action are a few tools of control.

Communicate

Much of successfully managing change entails strategically planning communications, which are the conduit between human perception and behaviors. The change-management role keeps people informed and on the right track, detailing the "who," "what," "when," and "how" of change. Champions of change include regular communications as part of their normal job responsibilities. As an added bonus, employees cite communication skills such as listening, giving and receiving feedback, and sharing information as qualities of effective managers.

The most effective communications are face-to-face, interpersonal interactions. Speaking with individuals personally or in small groups is an example. Personal communication conveys respect for people, encourages input and feedback, and allows for immediate clarification of misunderstandings or assumptions. Further, personal interaction allows for observation and interpretation of nonverbals, also called "body language," which may represent as much as 80 percent of all communications. Body language, particularly facial expressions, is a mirror to one's true feelings.

Written communications, whether formal or informal, do provide documentation that may leave a valuable paper trail. Letters and memoranda can be good vehicles for sharing data yet are limited in their effectiveness by virtue of their one-way nature. Although commonly used, e-mail is not an appropriate means of communication for important issues—and often contributes to negative environments. E-mail is an impersonal, one-way form of communication that often comes across as harsh, even insulting. How often have you questioned the intent, motivation, or content of e-mails you have received? We are more prone to respond to e-mails, however, than to letters or memoranda.

Establish Clear Goals and Expectations

Ambiguity often runs rampant in organizations, particularly when new ways of doing business are contemplated. Consider the times you started a new job or joined a different organization. What were the first few days like? Were you barraged with forms to complete, policies and procedures, the company tour, and then led from department to department and introduced to a sea of faces with whom you'd eventually interact? How unsettling were those experiences? And when did someone share with you the big and local pictures—the organization's vision and mission, departmental or unit goals, and how you fit in along with your specific expected contributions? More often than not, managers fail to effectively discuss clear goals and expectations of their employees. Change efforts are no different. We have many excuses: we're busy, the change was unexpected, employees should know, and so on.

Establishing clear goals and expectations *with* employees is the first step in performance management. Individual goals are the targets at which we aim; expectations outline the level of quality to which we perform. All should be directly aligned with unit, department, and organizational goals, mission, and vision. Collaboratively setting goals with employees increases their level of buy-in, clarifies their understanding of objectives, and helps ensure their ability to perform to expectations. Some are intimidated by the prospect of establishing goals for themselves and others, yet the process is rather simple. Effective goals are SMART: specific, measurable, attainable, results-oriented, and time-based.

Engage/Involve Others

Managers often feel as though they must provide all the answers. Fortunately, we are surrounded by talented, knowledgeable individuals who are typically eager to share their insights and opinions in meaningful ways. People like to be involved and appreciate being asked—it raises their self-esteem. Tapping the wealth of talent that surrounds us yields abundant benefits, from increased loyalty and productivity to teamwork (see Table 3.2).

Anticipate and Address Personnel Problems and Conflict

Change causes conflict—it is inevitable and unavoidable. Anyone who has been married, had a child, purchased a home, moved to a new location, started a new position, or received a promotion or transfer can attest to the disruption caused by even the most desirable change. Regrettably, most organizations are unrealistic about the amount of conflict that occurs

Table 3.2
Benefits of Employee Involvment

Benefits For Employees	Benefits For Managers	Benefits For Organizations
Allows people to make a contribution	Share the work	More engaged, productive workforce
Highlights ones knowledge, skills, and competencies	Assess employees' strengths and skills	Helps human resource planning
Enhances self-esteem	Increases loyalty and trust	Contributes to a collaborative culture
May position employee for recognition or rewards	Enhances teamwork and cooperation	Builds synergy
	Early employee involvement may pinpoint potential problems missed by management	The change stands a greater chance of success

and its impact on people. Quite logically, problems with personnel coincide with organizational conflict. Suppressing or denying conflict leads to dysfunctional behavior individually and organizationally, which impacts everyone. Since the best defense is a good offense, now is the time to anticipate and plan for personnel problems and the conflict that results.

How does a manager anticipate and plan for conflict? Although open communication is the key, the following guidelines are helpful in addressing the problems that conflict creates:

- Understand the physical and emotional impacts of change and stress on human beings.
- Understand that change and conflict are personal—treat individuals and their issues as unique.
- Provide a forum; publicly discuss the impending change and inevitable conflict.
- Ask those impacted what problems or conflict they foresee.
- Collaboratively explore potential solutions, approaches, and/or action plans to minimize the conflict.
- Encourage people to settle their differences and arrive at solutions in healthy, supportive ways.
- Keep lines of communication open; seek feedback.
- Constantly monitor the change, conflict, and people's reactions.
- Be flexible and open to ideas.
- Revisit the positives of the change and seek win-win solutions.
- Show appreciation for employee efforts, feedback, resolution of conflict, and results.

When the underlying difficulty is between employees, such as when conflict occurs between two or more individuals, successful problem solvers know when the problem is not theirs to solve. Occasionally, issues between and among people are personal or private (due to value differences, personality conflicts, etc.) and best resolved by the impacted parties. Individuals must be encouraged to settle their own differences, although occasional guidance or third-party objectivity may be valuable. A wise manager knows when to mediate and when to step back.

Recognize and Reward

Recognition and reward programs should be designed to help organizations achieve specific outcomes—such as change. Unfortunately, many managers and their organizations plan and implement change without altering their reward programs. One common reason for change-initiative failure is the belief by employees that they won't be rewarded for changing—or in fact will be punished (with more work, loss of status, job insecurity, etc.). In their criticism of recognition and rewards programs, individuals often state that

- they are not adequately rewarded for success in their current jobs (so why change?)
- they are punished with more work and higher goals when they are successful
- they are told to engage in—and rewarded for—less important work activities
- they are asked to do one thing (e.g., work as a team) but are rewarded for something else (e.g., individual performance)

Rewarding the "right" behaviors challenges many managers who face a myriad of organizational pressures on a daily basis. Times of change provide an excellent opportunity for organizations to review and update their recognition and reward programs to support any initiative. Care must be taken to align recognition and reward programs with organizational values, vision, mission, and goals.

Change managers have a different focus than change leaders; thus they desire and reward distinctly different behaviors. Managing change focuses on implementation and results; therefore, improved productivity, attitude (receptivity to change), loyalty and commitment, creativity, development of long-term solutions, and being a team player/cooperation are highly regarded during the change process. Managers are able to recognize and reward their employees in a variety of ways. The key is to provide employees with rewards that are personally meaningful to them. Since we are each motivated differently, managers must discover the personal reasons and motivators that stimulate our desire to change or excel.

Recognition and rewards may be nonmonetary or monetary. Nonmonetary forms include appreciation (ranked as the number-one motivator of employees) and genuine praise, which are free of charge yet valuable to those on the receiving end. Individuals may be motivated by special assignments, challenging work, the opportunity to be creative, employee-of-the-month status, social gatherings, casual-dress days, time off or "comp time," plaques, food, and so forth. The list is as endless and unique as the people with whom we work. Managers who complain that they have no funds or budget with which to reward their personnel lack understanding of the factors that prompt people to excel. Understanding the distinctive personality and motivators of employees makes a manager's efforts to recognize and reward much easier.

Monetary rewards—cash or its equivalent—are powerful motivators for some, particularly for rewards of significant size. Most of us, however, are limited in budget and scope; therefore, acceptable rewards are often proportionate to the accomplishment or constrained by company policy and procedures. Common monetary rewards include cash, gift certificates or cards, and prizes. Sales and marketing organizations sometimes bestow trips, extra vacation days, or lavish gifts (Rolex watches, stays in the corporate condo) on their best performers. Group rewards often include bonuses, outings (golf, amusement park, sporting events), group lunches, or something tangible yet symbolic of the accomplishment (e.g., the traveling "superstar" trophy).

Make Change Last

As with the human body, organizations respond to change without exception. Unlike the human body, many organizations and their employees (at all levels, from executives to the front line) fail to even tolerate change. For many, change invokes an instant, *defensive* response that recedes only upon defeat of the change via overt or covert methods.

How do we prevent rejection and encourage people and their organizations to accept desired change and permanently alter their behaviors?

1. Include anchoring the change in your plan.
2. Continually stress the benefits of change and the dangers of failure to change.
3. Reward individuals and groups for their change efforts, and celebrate victories.
4. Disarm the sentinels of the immune system: engage them in the process; reassign.
5. Work to create a culture of change.

CONCLUSION

The increasingly complex world of business, compounded by the rate of change, forces managers to continually examine their positions and functions, resulting in the adoption and integration of several new and exciting roles and responsibilities. Change leadership challenges traditional thinking while offering a dynamic approach to developing high-performing people and organizations.

FOUR

Skills and Competencies of a Change Leader

One change makes way for the next, giving us the opportunity to grow.

—Vivian Buchan

Recognizing and understanding leadership and management functions does not guarantee success—a variety of skills, ability, knowledge, and aptitude are needed to implement change well. For example, a marketing manager may know technical skills such as pricing, market research, advertising, and sales techniques yet may be ineffective as a manager or leader of people. Managers may rely less on basic technical skills as they rise within an organization, yet these skills provide the foundation for their new responsibilities and an appreciation for the work of those around them.

Seven broad dimensions form a framework of the specific skills, experiences, and requirements of change leadership. These are leadership skills, management skills, problem solving and decision making, interpersonal skills, communications, change-process and implementation skills, and business and general knowledge. The specific knowledge, skills, and competencies within each broad category are by no means mutually exclusive to each dimension—they often overlap. For example, interpersonal and

Table 4.1
Roles, Responsibilities, Skills, and Competencies of a Change Leader

Roles	Responsibilities	Knowledge/ Skill / Competency
Visionary	Challenge the Status Quo	Risk-taker Business knowledge (industry, company, people, products) Problem solver Persuasive Confident Adaptable Results-driven
	Imagine the Future	Ability to visualize Creative Tolerant of ambiguity
	Philosophy of Stewardship	Accountable Ability to put the needs of others above your own
	Align the Change	Strategic Alliance builder
	Share the Vision	Articulate
Inspirer	Sell the Change	Persuasive Sell the benefits Passionate
	Involve Others	Build alliances Engaging
	Model the Change	Genuine Walk the talk
Supporter	Create a Culture of Change	Identify and remove barriers to change Trust others Allow mistakes Flexible Open – minded Encourage feedback
	Secure Resources	Business acumen Understand organizational politics, processes, policies
	Involve Others	Collaborative Build alliances Trust Delegate Coach

Table 4.1
(continued)

Roles	Responsibilities	Knowledge/ Skill / Competency
	Encourage Creativity and Innovation	Trust Provide resources and a safe environment
	Communicate	Articulate Knowledge of communication processes Active listening Feedback
	Own the Change	Visibly responsible Accountable
	Model the Behavior	Genuine Walk the talk
	Enhance Own Skills	Lifelong learner Adaptable Understand own limitations
	Recognize and Reward	Understand motivation techniques; human behavior
Problem Solver	Analyze the Situation	Ability to gather data via multiple means Analytical Generate and evaluate alternatives
	Craft Solutions	Creative, innovative Resourceful Results-driven
	Monitor	Personal involvement Evaluate
Change Manager	Coordinate Change	Knowledge of change processes (planning, facilitation, management) Able to identify and remove barriers to change
	Communicate	Articulate Knowledge of communication methods Active listening Feedback
	Establish Clear Goals and Expectations	Results-driven Knowledge of goal setting and motivation techniques
	Involve Others	Trust others Delegate Value the contributions of others
	Anticipate and Address Personnel Problems	Knowledge of human behavior Manage resistance

(continued)

**Table 4.1
(continued)**

Roles	Responsibilities	Knowledge/ Skill / Competency
	Manage Conflict	Conflict management Negotiate Mediate
	Recognize and Reward	Understand motivation techniques Knowledge of human behavior
	Make Change Last	Knowledge of human behavior and motivation techniques

change-process skills both require knowledge of basic human behavior. See Table 4.1 for contrasts and comparisons of the skills and competencies vital to each role of a change leader.

Some view change-leadership skills as similar to essential core-management skills—and they are correct. Change agency *is* a core-management skill and particularly in demand within dynamic organizations. Successful change leaders are able to make sense of change contexts and then deploy knowledge and core competencies appropriately. No two change scenarios are exactly the same; hence the requisite combination of one's skills and competencies are unique to each situation.

LEADERSHIP SKILLS

Leadership skills are at the forefront of change—they are the manifestation of influential traits and behaviors that act as a catalyst for change. No two leaders are the same, nor is their combination of unique knowledge, skills, and abilities. Research reveals the following are possessed by change leaders:

Risk-taker	**Problem Solver**
Articulate	Strategic
Persuasive	Adaptable
Passionate	Business Acumen
Able to Visualize	Alliance Builder
Confident	Tolerant of Ambiguity
Creative	Able to Manage Stress
Engaging	Accountable
Results-driven	Able to Remove Barriers

Risk Taker

A risk is an element of danger or probability of loss.[1] Change leaders have an above-average tolerance of risk that enables them to challenge the status quo in favor of future gains. By definition, change propels us into the unknown, thus entailing a degree of risk and uncertainty. Change leaders are willing to put themselves—often their reputations, even careers—on the line in search of meaningful change. General Colin Powell, former secretary of state, is known for his willingness to undertake the risky business of challenging the status quo.

Articulate

The most effective change leaders share a vision that is concise and memorable, capturing the essence of what the organization is striving to achieve. I've worked with firms whose vision, mission, and goals are complex, intricate, well-worded dissertations spanning multiple pages drafted by savvy executive teams. Unfortunately, few employees are familiar with these corporate statements, and even fewer understand the gist of where they are supposed to be headed.

An articulate change champion shares a simple message of hope, direction, and success—one that appeals to the hearts and minds of members at all levels of the organization. Leaders bring their visions to life through stories, symbols, and metaphors that clearly connect with their audience. Ross Perot was known for his strong articulation of his vision for EDS; similarly, Ronald Reagan was known for his skillful ability to communicate and articulate.

Persuasive

Change leaders have a strong need for power because they want to influence others to accomplish goals that benefit the organization. Although we each are influenced by slightly different appeals, we are drawn to individuals whose thoughts, goals, and ideals are similar to ours. Change leaders make the effort to understand our passions and preferences and filter their appeals to us through this knowledge.

Change efforts require leaders to empathize with others, build rapport, and network. These social skills channel the leader's message and draw us in.

Passionate

Servant leaders demonstrate passionate enthusiasm for change and encourage passion in organizational members. Individual passion drives motivation and performance, focusing one's efforts on accomplishment of the objective. A leader's passion may inspire his or her followers, drawing them in and feeding their ambitions. Similarly, nourishing passion in others taps into their spirit and frees them to excel.

Unbridled passion, as with anything in excess, may pose problems. People may become obsessive, unbending, or narrow, so caught up in the issue or event that they are blind to reality. Many myths abound about passion; here are a few:

- Passion is always good.
- Passion is emotion out of control.
- Passion isn't appropriate in a professional firm.
- Actions intended to improve the situation will always evoke positive passions.

Able to Visualize

The ability to define the future is often associated with sheer brilliance and years of experience. Michael Dell and Bill Gates are two examples of men who saw a reality different from others in the computer business—and did so at a relatively young age. Dell dropped out of college to start a build-to-order personal computer business that defied the conventional wisdom prevalent in the IBMs of the world. Gates, a self-acknowledged geek in high school, was determined to make using a computer as easy as "point and click." He built the world's most successful software company and in the process became the richest man in America. These men refused to be constrained by "what is," instead preferring to envision "what could be." They described the future for themselves and their organizations in ways others had never considered and, in doing so, changed the world of business.

Many accomplished athletes use visualization techniques prior to competition. Michael Jordan and Jack Nicklaus, for example, visualize their successful performance before the event and then turn that vision into reality. Visualization of the future is not always clear or precise, which makes comfort with ambiguity critical.

Do not confuse visualization with fantasy. Visualization entails mentally modeling performance, focusing on the positive—sometimes incremental—steps necessary to achieve acceptable results given the capabilities and constraints of oneself and the organization. Visualization skills improve with practice, reflection, and engagement of multiple senses (sight, hearing, touch, and so forth).

Confident

Leaders believe in their skills and abilities, and it shows. They also express confidence in those around them, convinced of the power of positive thinking. Self-assurance enables them to face adversity with courage, even if they are not completely successful. Change leaders understand that failure, in fact, teaches us more than success—for we reflect on our failures, agonize over and analyze them, and become stronger and more competent as a result of this learning. Carly Fiorina, former CEO of Hewlett-Packard Co., is known for her confidence.

Creative

Envisioning what does not yet exist tests even the most inventive mind. Undaunted, however, change leaders persevere, sometimes motivated by the challenge of developing unusual or unconventional alternatives.

Creative individuals are dissatisfied with the status quo and seek new and exciting solutions to problems. They are sometimes perceived as difficult or renegade, and their approaches are not always welcomed by traditional firms. Given the need for fast-paced decisions, however, an organization's ability to stimulate creativity and innovation may sow the seeds of success. Change leaders develop creative environments by

- encouraging others to be open to new ideas and experiences
- allowing employees to have fun
- treating mistakes and failures as learning opportunities
- rewarding creative endeavors

Engaging

Involve people at all levels early and often. Change is best tackled on all fronts by tapping the collective wisdom and experience of organizational members new and old.

Many change managers engage employees in the implementation phase, long after the initial decisions have been made. This shortsighted approach denies the value of potential contributions by well-meaning people at all levels. This is also where resistance takes hold—when individuals are told to execute plans with which they've had no input.

Successful change leaders recognize the talent within their firms and encourage (and reward) the involvement of these individuals. Engaging others requires trust, the ability to delegate, active listening, and a safe forum for expression. Although participation and involvement are not cure-alls for resistance to change, they certainly have their place in change strategy.

Results-Driven

Change without focus is time, effort, and resources wasted. Well-planned change focuses on achieving specific results, within a certain timeframe, that improve the state of the organization and its stakeholders. Occasionally, some organizational leaders and managers become so desperate for or enamored of the potential promise of change that they devote their energies to the process of change, to the detriment of results.

Problem Solver

Superior ability to gather and analyze information, identify and evaluate alternative scenarios, and recommend viable solutions to complex problems is a valuable skill. Problem solving requires attention to detail, thorough knowledge of the organization and its capabilities, creativity, and a certain amount of risk. Jack Welch, former CEO of General Electric, is known for his ability to make tough decisions.

Strategic

Strategy outlines an organization's long-term direction and actions, including changes, required to achieve planned results. Leaders are strategic when they hold a global, "big picture" perspective of an organization coupled with an understanding of the interrelatedness of its numerous parts. Change must align with the organization's vision, mission, values, and goals while concurrently shaping them. This congruence "narrows the gap between strategy and performance."[2]

A strategic approach to change appreciates that change creates change, causes a ripple effect, and may yield solutions that are tomorrow's problems. Change leaders anticipate and plan for this eventuality.

Adaptable

There is a saying about "best laid plans" that proves so true. In spite of our detailed plans and enthusiastic hopes, there are no guarantees. For this reason, leaders of change are adaptable to shifting conditions. Encounters with the unexpected reveal gaps in our strategy, talent, and/or implementation. Occasionally, changing conditions highlight our strengths and organizational opportunities. Either way, we are forced to regroup and refocus our efforts. Change leaders are sensitive to situational cues and readily adapt their own behavior to the people and circumstances.

The U.S. auto industry learned a hard lesson in the 1970s and 1980s when it failed to respond to changes in Japanese manufacturing and marketing. At least two decades passed before the quality of American cars was perceived to be competitive with that of the Japanese. Conversely, 3M seized an opportunity with Post-It notes, the result of trials of adhesives of varying strengths. A less-adaptive scientist wouldn't have recognized the potential. Change agents, similarly, are flexible, responsive, and open to opportunities posed by changes in the internal and external environments.

Business Acumen

Leaders need to understand the business environment in which they operate at the global, industry, regional, local, company, and product levels. Effectively proposing and implementing change requires the ability to process enormous amounts of information. This isn't genius; rather, it is the ability to make sense of varied and complex information that yields clues to yet unseen trends or potential opportunities. Business savvy enables change leaders to recognize opportunities and strategize means by which to capture them. See "Business and General Knowledge" later in this chapter.

Alliance Builder

Just as it "takes a village" to raise a child, it takes teams of people working in concert to execute and sustain change. Champions of change build partnerships and coalitions of individuals dedicated to the change effort by appealing to the needs and emotions of supporters.

Tolerant of Ambiguity

The first glimpse of the future often seems unclear, even ludicrous. Horseless carriages, flight, a man on the moon, home computers, picture phones—these current realities were the stuff of science fiction not so long ago. The ability to straddle the edge of current reality in quest of the future demands that change leaders release their grip on the present and leap into the unknown. Although the Wright brothers suspected that flight was possible for man, given their research and observations, they didn't *know* until their test flight in Kitty Hawk. They took the risk, unsure of the outcome, and continued to build on their successes and failures. Change leaders have a high tolerance for ambiguity, for they really have no choice. The future is always in motion and sometimes quite elusive.

Able to Manage Stress

Stress, although caused by many factors, is one's response to a situation that is perceived as challenging or threatening to one's well-being.

Change is often that situation. Physiological symptoms of stress include a faster heartbeat, sweaty hands, higher blood pressure, feelings of exhaustion, inability to sleep, even ulcers. Emotional and behavioral symptoms include resistance, avoidance, impatience, loss of temper, and being argumentative. Stress leads to lower job satisfaction, higher absenteeism, workplace aggression, and job burnout. In response, some people react by actively fighting or running away—the "fight or flight response."[3] Those who engage in a control strategy attempt to anticipate or solve problems proactively, while ignoring or avoiding the situation amounts to escapism.

Clearly, change is stressful, and leading change may be more so, for champions of change must manage their own stress and deal with the issues of other people. Fortunately, there are many ways to manage stress; however, given the personal nature of change and stress, what works for some may not work for others. We each must develop our own tool kit of coping strategies. A few examples include

- meditation and other relaxation techniques (e.g., breathing)
- biofeedback
- breaks and vacations
- flexible work time
- work broken down into small, manageable increments
- discussion groups/meetings to discuss problems as they arise
- exercise and nutrition
- hobbies
- empowering others to have more control over their work

Many people exercise before or after work, read a book during their lunch hour, or lose themselves in hobbies (actress Julia Roberts knits between filming) to relieve stress. Leaders and managers can help their employees lessen stress by providing adequate training and resources, providing forums (e.g., weekly meetings) for discussing work problems and potential solutions, and empowering them to take more control of their work and work environment.

These techniques tend to relieve symptoms of stress rather than eliminate the causes. Consequently, results may be temporary or inconsistent depending on the depth and scope of the stress.

Accountable

True leaders take responsibility and hold themselves accountable for the success of their people and initiatives. They translate words into deeds by championing the change, providing the tools for success, staying on course, and thereby legitimizing the change. Change leaders walk the talk, exhibiting behaviors that symbolize values and expectations, particularly of themselves. For them the change is personal and "the buck stops here." They initiated the change—they will see it to fruition.

Providing the resources necessary to do the job is an important component of accountability. Lack of sufficient resources to accomplish required tasks is a common complaint of employees and their managers, particularly during tight economic times. Change leaders understand that following a different path calls for additional, sometimes unique input; consequently, they fight for and secure the resources and tools necessary for their people and organizations to achieve success.

Remove Barriers to Change

Change will not occur as planned unless its barriers are identified and removed. Barriers to change often include dysfunctional policies and procedures, inadequate resources, ineffective managers, negative employees, and poor communications. These barriers to change contribute to a culture that prevents change rather than supports it.

MANAGEMENT SKILLS

By definition, managers are responsible for organizing activities within their realm of control. Management skills put change into action; hence they are critical to the success of change.

The traditional perception of management includes planning, directing, organizing, and controlling. Keep in mind that people can be led, not successfully managed (or micromanaged). Management skills are effective with things (such as budgets and resources), processes, and procedures. People demand personal interaction; thus we include communication and evaluation as critical change-management skills.

Self-Management	Organize
Able to Add Value	Control
Plan	Communicate
Results-Driven*	Evaluate
*Discussed previously	

Self-Management

Personal management skills such as management of one's time, neatness and arrangement of one's desk and office, and preparedness for meetings and projects are particularly important during change initiatives. Unorganized managers tend to let things fall through the cracks and quickly lose the respect of their colleagues and staff. The office of the academic vice president for a small, private university was called "the black hole"—she was notorious for having mountains of paperwork scattered around her office and the tendency to misplace documents. Experience taught people to mistrust her handling of important papers.

Able to Add Value

Management is more than simply guiding or controlling the actions of others. Effective managers approach work relationships with their subordinates as partnerships in which each party contributes to the success of the overall engagement. Adding value involves contributing your knowledge, experience, and expertise in ways that benefit your employees, peers, superiors, and the organization. Your absence or loss would be noticeable and, even more, detrimental to the success of the change.

Plan, Organize, Control

Planning answers "who," "how," and "when" long-term and short-term actions will be implemented. Planning begins with the end result in mind and works backward from the anticipated deadline. Change leaders as managers identify the talent (who), necessary learning, resources, and actions (how), and timelines (when) requisite to make the change happen.

Organizing involves arranging and coordinating the people, resources, and actions identified in the planning phase. Any change initiative can get out of control quickly, which makes organization and control imperative. Constant monitoring tracks the progress of change and allows for alterations in course should difficulties in the plan arise.

Communicate

Communication skills are vital, regardless of one's position. Change management compels managers to encourage two-way, frequent interactions throughout the process, from planning to evaluation. Effective communication involves frequent soundings, or feedback, throughout the change process and with all stakeholders. See previous discussions of communication for more information.

Evaluate

At some point the results of change must be assessed. Measuring the impact of change requires exacting appraisal of individual and organizational learning, behavior change, and outcomes to obtain evidence that the organization has improved as a result of the initiative. Change leaders incorporate evaluation strategies into the master plan.

PROBLEM-SOLVING AND DECISION-MAKING SKILLS

These skills involve one's ability to examine and understand complex issues along with the numerous factors that influence these issues, problems, or opportunities, and solve problems in ways that maximize potential benefits for the organization and its stakeholders. Experience, instinct, cognitive ability, and resourcefulness influence the development of these skills.

> Knowledge of Capabilities and Weaknesses
> Collaborative
> Investigative and Analytical Skills
> Ability to Generate Alternatives
> Results-Driven*
>
> *Discussed previously

Knowledge of Capabilities and Weaknesses

Informed decision making and problem solving begin with a comprehensive understanding of the capabilities and weaknesses of the organization and its members. Organizational capabilities such as executive and management talent, resource availability, culture, resilience, responsiveness, market position, and technology are but a few of the variables that must be considered in making educated, viable decisions. Change leaders are acutely aware of the assets and liabilities within their realms.

Collaborative

A participative approach indicates a shift from authoritarian domination. Participation and collaboration require change leaders to have the courage to relinquish control. A collaborative style yields many advantages, among them are the following:

- organizational synergy
- improved diagnosis
- increased support of and cooperation for decisions
- better relationships due to mutual trust and respect
- improved results

Investigative and Analytical Skills

Problem solvers and decision makers rely on their curiosity, intuition, and investigative skills to uncover root causes, effects, capabilities, limitations, and any other influencers of impending decisions. This research includes dialoguing with others, asking questions, taking surveys, observing, and any other ethical means by which one gathers data.

Change leaders are challenged to assess people, behaviors, situations, opportunities, processes, the competition, the environment, and so forth. The ability to evaluate and make sense of copious and complex data, and use the results to frame effective decision making is, therefore, a valuable skill. Although a complex skill, the *process* of problem solving is rather straightforward:

1. Gather data—via observation, surveys, historical records, and so forth.
2. Organize findings—compile facts and evidence.
3. Draw conclusions—based on verifiable evidence, what is the current problem?
4. Generate and assess alternative solutions—brainstorm multiple solutions, then evaluate the viability of each with respect to organizational culture, individual and organizational talent and capabilities, willingness to change, cost, time constraints, and so forth.
5. Recommend viable alternative(s)—based on the above analysis, which, if any, alternatives will work?

Ability to Generate and Assess Alternatives

Once again, creativity surfaces as a desired component of a larger skill set—testimony to the significance of one's ability to innovate, think outside the box, and develop alternative solutions to complicated problems or scenarios. Resourceful change leaders generate options by freeing their imaginations and thought processes of the constraints of traditional thinking. An understanding of relevant capabilities and weaknesses, paired with in-depth investigation and analysis, provides the solid foundation on which alternatives may be generated and evaluated for viability.

INTERPERSONAL SKILLS

Interpersonal skills, often called "people skills," influence one's ability to work well with others. Managers typically spend the majority of their time interacting with people; therefore, they must cultivate their ability to communicate effectively with the diversity of individuals around them. In many companies, the reason managers fail is due to a lack of people skills. Effective managers focus on interpersonal skills such as sharing information, providing appropriate feedback, coaching, being a team player, and helping people learn. Their understanding of change, human nature, and motivation techniques enables them to generate superior results with their people.

Adaptable*	Motivation Techniques
Flexible	Coaching
Collaborative*	Conflict Resolution
Knowledge of Human Nature	
*Discussed in previous section	

Flexible

What doesn't bend might break; therefore, champions of change strive for flexibility in themselves and others in their approach to and implementation of change. Flexibility does not imply weakness or inability to make decisions. On the contrary, flexibility reveals one's awareness, responsiveness, and sensitivity to change; stakeholder needs; and individual and organizational capabilities.

Knowledge of Human Nature

Human beings are complex individuals, each unique yet often possessing similar characteristics or predispositions. Successful managers understand the principles of human nature such as our inherent resistance to change, need for feedback, or desire for involvement in decision making. This information they combine with the understanding of the uniqueness of each individual to form a solid knowledge base of human behavior. Armed with information, managers experience greater success in executing change.

Understanding of Motivation Techniques

Motivation is the force that inspires us to act. Motivation is very personal and uniquely our own—there is no one-size-fits-all strategy that yields success. We are each motivated by different things, such as prestige, recognition, freedom, challenge, security, money, and so forth. The key is to discover what motivates each individual and align his or her needs with opportunities presented by the change. For example, the change might offer a chance for promotion, highly visible work, challenge, or the opportunity to lead, among others.

Uncovering one's specific motivators is a task easily accomplished via observation and questioning—ask what motivates him or her. Armed with this information, managers are able to establish conditions that are motivating for their staff, resulting in stronger interpersonal relationships and more effective implementation of change.

Do not assume that all people are motivated primarily by money, for research indicates they are not. In fact, in most employee surveys cash ranks between fourth and eighth in terms of importance—appreciation typically ranks as most important.

Coaching

Gone are the days when managers devoted their time to planning, directing, organizing, and controlling. Today's sophisticated workplace and employees demand more of their managers—from training and career guidance to mentoring and creation of healthy work environments. In short, managers must stop managing and start coaching.[4] Performance coaching enhances interpersonal relationships as managers train and mentor their employees, provide feedback and confront poor performance, and engage in career counseling. Activities such as these promote synergistic relationships and trust, while enhancing interpersonal skills and relationships.

Conflict Resolution

Change is a common driver of organizational life. "As a result, confronting difficult issues is critical for change leaders because much of their work consists of exposing issues that organizational members are reluctant to face. A change champion must work proactively to both prevent unnecessary conflict and aggressively resolve the inevitable conflicts that do arise."[5]

The process for resolving conflicts includes acknowledgment, clarification, problem solving, and taking action.

1. Acknowledge the conflict—recognize that it exists and is important to the affected parties.
2. Clarify—uncover the heart of the problem, the root cause. Understanding the full context of an interpersonal or intergroup conflict begins with examination of the underlying causes of the friction. The issue or situation typically represents the overt façade of the conflict. The true source of the conflict lies deep within us—and these factors must be exposed and addressed. Table 4.2 illustrates some of the hidden causes of conflict.
3. Problem solve—collaboratively generate options, evaluate alternatives, and recommend a viable solution(s).
4. Take action—plan and set the recommendation in motion.

Conflict resolution requires an understanding of human nature and why conflict occurs, how to respond accordingly, and how to guide people to agreement. People are inherently resistant to change and being changed; thus conflict is inevitable. The source may be contradictory or incompatible goals, values, ideas, personalities, policies and procedures, and so on (see Table 4.2, Hidden Causes of Conflict). Dealing with conflict requires change leaders to be proficient in (1) understanding conflict and resolution processes, (2) guiding honest, nonjudgmental discussion and feedback, (3) negotiation (reaching compromise), (4) mediation (bringing people together to work through their issues), (5) confronting poor performance, and (6) implementing resolutions.

Although a natural component of the change process, conflict can be messy and sometimes painful. We cannot eliminate conflict, but we can work through it—even learn from it. Also see "Conflict Management" later in this chapter.

Table 4.2
Hidden Causes of Conflict

Issue or Situation
egos
personalities
emotions
interests
wants and needs
perceptions
expectations
unresolved past issues

COMMUNICATION SKILLS

Communication is simply the sharing of information between two or more individuals. The process represents the conduit via which information flows through channels between a sender and a receiver—a message is encoded, transmitted, received, and decoded. The sender encodes a message with words, gestures, symbols or other signs, then transmits to the receiver through one or more communication channels. The receiver decodes the message through his or her own filters, the meaning of which may or may not reflect what the sender intended. How can such a simple process go wrong?

The transmission of meaning from person to person may be hampered by numerous barriers, including differences in perceptions or language (ambiguity, jargon, etc.), information overload or scarcity, cultural influences, stereotypes, biases, and lack of understanding of communications processed by managers and employees, to name a few. Add the stress and uncertainty associated with change, and many communications efforts are often anemic, at best.

Change leaders may improve their communications by seeking feedback regarding the sent message, sharing needed information in a timely fashion, using methods (letters, memoranda, e-mail, face-to-face discussions) that are appropriate to the importance of the message, understanding and compensating for biases and other differences, understanding the communications needs of receivers, and incorporating communications into their strategic change plan.

Active Listening	Two-Way Interaction
Understanding of Communication Channels	

Active Listening

Many of us hear but fail to listen—we are cognizant of sound or noise, but often neglect to pay attention to messages intended for us. Active listening requires concentration on our part in order to absorb and comprehend the meaning of messages. Active listening involves giving our undivided attention to the sender, looking him or her in the eye, concentrating on the message being shared, and confirming our understanding.

Two-Way Interaction

Effective communicators encourage input from both parties—they are not afraid of comments, opinions, or divergent views of stakeholders. Champions of change promote open, two-way communications to

- enhance trust
- solicit employee input on the feasibility and potential problems of change efforts
- increase cooperation, involvement, and buy-in
- alert to barriers, roadblocks

Understanding of Communication Channels

The channel through which information is transmitted may be verbal or nonverbal. Verbal communications are any oral or written method of transmitting meaning through words. Nonverbal communication, which comprises an estimated 80 percent of communications, does not use words and consists primarily of body language.

Oral communications, particularly one-on-ones and group meetings, are most effective because they allow senders and receivers to assess voice tone and inflection along with body language. For this reason, face-to-face interactions are effective for conveying emotions and persuading receivers.

Written communications in the form of letters or memoranda may provide an abundance of information and are more effective for transmitting technical details or large amounts of data. E-mail is quick and may be efficient, yet is frequently overused and therefore abused. E-mails are often hastily composed, fraught with errors, frequently misinterpreted, and seem harsh. Because of its casual nature, e-mail is not an effective means of communicating important information. A multifaceted approach including well-planned oral and written communications proves most effective.

CHANGE PROCESSES AND IMPLEMENTATION

The heart of continuous improvement and organizational long-term viability is change. Hence, the need for managers who possess change-implementation skills is greater than ever. So, too, is the challenge. In an interview with *Fast Company* magazine, Peter Senge, a well-known author on the subject of change, says, "there's enough evidence of success to say that change is possible—and enough evidence of failure to say that it isn't likely."[6]

The ability to successfully plan and execute change separates effective change leaders from ordinary managers.

<table>
<tr><td>Change Processes</td><td>Conflict Management*</td><td>Stress Management*</td></tr>
<tr><td>Remove Barriers*</td><td>Motivation*</td><td>Collaborative*</td></tr>
<tr><td>Negotiation</td><td>Adaptable*</td><td>Results-Driven*</td></tr>
<tr><td>Communications*</td><td></td><td></td></tr>
</table>

*Discussed in previous section

Knowledge of Change Processes

Change is a continuous process, not a one-time event. Unfortunately, many firms attempt to undertake radical change in a relatively short span of time and behave as if this one change will revolutionize the business and secure the future. A vast amount of time and resources is dedicated to the initiative, with promises that "we'll get through this." Treating change as a rare, unique episode to be tackled with exhaustive fervor amid promises of a desirable end ignores the true nature of change and misleads those who are involved. Change is constant, as should be our approach.

Change involves learning; therefore, employees should be provided with new information incrementally, over time, and allowed to practice in a safe environment. Input from impacted employees encourages buy-in and may provide insight into potential problems or additional benefits of the change. Communications are essential, as is an understanding of the impact of change on individuals. We each react differently; have varying tolerances for change, ambiguity, and stress; and have our own unique predisposition toward change. Working through change is a distinctly personal experience requiring change leaders who understand the complexities of change, human reactions, and ways to collaboratively reach success.

Conflict Management

Conflict is an unavoidable component of organizational life, driven by constant change, increased competition, greater diversity of employees, scarcity of resources, globalization and cross-cultural influences, more technology (and less interpersonal communication), communication problems, and emphasis on teams. Fortunately, conflict isn't all bad. Appropriate levels of conflict can be energizing, resulting in new solutions and improved performance.

Dysfunctional levels of conflict occur when too little or too much conflict is present. Organizations, divisions, or units devoid of conflict are plagued by lack of creativity and responsiveness, apathy, and indecision. Excessive conflict, conversely, destroys morale and teamwork, causes job dissatisfaction and turnover, and may lead to aggression or violence in the workplace.

Conflict occurs when "one party perceives its interests are being opposed or negatively affected by another party."[7] Once again, communication is a key tool in managing conflict. Tjosvold's cooperative conflict model describes three desirable outcomes of conflict:

1. Agreement—Equitable and fair agreements in which all parties feel well-represented.
2. Stronger relationships—just agreements and resolution of differences permit conflicting parties to find common ground and build trust.
3. Learning—Functional conflict can promote creativity, problem solving, and development of new approaches that contribute to the individual and collective knowledge base. Any process is learned by doing, and experience is a valuable teacher.[8]

Also see previous discussion of conflict resolution.

Negotiation

Negotiation is the give-and-take process of reaching agreement. Everyone negotiates, almost daily. We negotiate sale prices and delivery dates, project assignments, resource allocation—even where to have lunch with coworkers. Negotiation skills are important in resolving conflict and moving change forward.

Although a win-win approach that emphasizes benefits to all would be ideal, it is not always realistic. Occasionally, someone must relinquish or even lose to some degree. Our challenge is to balance losses with acceptable gains, often through compromise, accommodation, or collaboration. The desired outcome is a result that all parties embrace as meeting their needs. Compromise and accommodation are considered win-lose scenarios in that each party generally gives up something in exchange for something else. Collaboration, a win-win style, is based on trust and cooperation—elements often missing in conflict situations.

BUSINESS AND GENERAL KNOWLEDGE

Change leaders aren't necessarily brilliant. They do, however, possess a broad understanding of the environment in which they work. Much of this knowledge flows from experience, pure and simple. Success and, more profoundly, failure are powerful teachers. Innate intelligence, instinct, and education are contributing factors.

External environment (industry, legal, societal)
Internal environment (company politics, practices, capabilities, weaknesses)
General knowledge
Personal strengths and weaknesses

External Environment

No organization operates free of the influence of external factors. Competition, legal constraints, societal pressures and trends, and more frame the environment in which businesses function. External factors present opportunities and threats, a thorough understanding of which enables leaders to make informed decisions.

Internal Environment

The organization's internal environment is characterized by its strengths and weaknesses, manifested in its politics, practices, human talent, products, responsiveness, and so forth. Many leaders have lengthy tenure with their organization—over the years they have learned who holds the power, the unwritten rules, and how to get things done. Knowledge is power, and power is influence.

General Knowledge

Individuals often possess an area of expertise—such as sales, accounting, marketing, manufacturing, or production—that serves as the foundation for their knowledge and experience. Effective leaders have expanded on this initial base and broadened their scope of knowledge, and thus, influence. We are often impressed by their network of business contacts, influence with local and regional power brokers, grasp of details as well as the big picture, and ability to blend people and processes in complex arrays focused on a common theme. Nora Ruder, vice president of Foremost Insurance, for example, combines her knowledge of the insurance industry, the company, products, finance, human behavior and motivation, sales, marketing, and buyer behavior, among others, to successfully lead her division. As a result, she possesses a great deal of credibility and influence within Foremost and the community.

Personal Strengths and Weaknesses

Effective leaders understand their own strengths and weaknesses and the impact these have on their performance and interaction with others. They take steps to maximize their strong points and minimize shortcomings by

- reflecting on and learning from successes and failures
- engaging in professional development
- surrounding themselves with persons with complementary skills
- seeking and acting on feedback (and coaching) from others

Recognizing our limitations frees us to involve and value the contributions of others. As a result, we seem more normal, approachable, and worthy of others' trust. Although admitting one's weaknesses can be a humbling experience, true leaders don't expect perfection in themselves or others. Perfection is an elusive, unrealistic ideal. Leaders who disclose their flaws and allow imperfection in others gain our respect and are often perceived as being even more exceptional.

CONCLUSION

Effective change leaders are immensely qualified, competent individuals. They possess a multitude of knowledge, skills, and competencies that enable them to successfully implement change. These include leadership, management, communications, problem solving, and interpersonal skills, coupled with a broad understanding of business and change processes.

PART II

Action Plan, Tools, and Resources

FIVE

Self-Assessment and Development

It is characteristic of living systems to continuously renew themselves.

—Margaret Wheatley

Most of us are "works in process." Whether we realize it or not, learning occurs on a daily basis as a result of our personal and professional experiences. We tend to learn more from our mistakes or failures, however, than from our successes. Why? Failure often rocks our world. We reflect on, re-examine, and agonize over our mistakes, often vowing not to make them again. We ask ourselves the following questions:

- How did this happen?
- What did I do wrong?
- Why did I make this decision?
- What can I do differently in the future?

Success doesn't have the same impact. Rarely do we reflect on the reasons for our successes—the conditions and sequence of decisions that resulted in our accomplishments. We triumph, congratulate ourselves, and move on without identifying the knowledge and skills we applied or the steps in which we engaged. As a result, we are often unable to duplicate our accidental successes, for we don't understand why they occurred.

Effective change leaders are analysts—curious about their environment, business, selves, and others—and constantly seeking ways to be more effective. As individuals improve their talents and abilities—that is, grow and develop—so, too, will their organizations. Just as we analyze organizations and create plans for improvement, we are able to assess our knowledge, skills, and abilities, and create action plans for our own development. This chapter includes self-assessment instruments and an action plan for self-development template that will allow you to evaluate your skills in various areas related to change leadership, then formulate a plan for improvement.

SELF-ASSESSMENT

The more self-awareness a person has, the more alive he is.

—Rollo May

Two self-assessment instruments are offered next. The Change-Leadership Characteristics summary reflects the most common characteristics employees desire in their leaders. This instrument has a *self-assessment* version along with an *assessment by others*. The most accurate evaluation of your skills will be the result of multiple inputs. Seek honest feedback from your colleagues and employees, and use this information to create your own self-development plan. This instrument may certainly be modified to reflect additional characteristics deemed important by you, your colleagues, or employees.

The Change-Leadership Competency Questionnaire provides a comprehensive examination of your knowledge, skills, and abilities that closely mirrors the competencies described in chapters 3 and 4. Once again, solicit input from those with whom you work closely and use their responses to frame your personal growth.

CHANGE-LEADERSHIP CHARACTERISTICS—
SELF-ASSESSMENT

Indicate the frequency with which **you** *demonstrate the following critical change-leadership characteristics.*

Characteristic	Rarely	Sometimes	Usually
Visionary			
Good listener			
Respects others			
Analytical			
Dependable			
Has a sense of humor			
Empathetic / caring			
Exhibits integrity			
Risk-taker			
Rewards/recognizes/ appreciates others			
Provides others with opportunities for growth			
Creative thinker			
Sets a good example / models desired behavior			
Inspiring			
Consistent			
Accountable			
Values diversity			
Servant to others			
Involves / engages others			
Fair			
Intelligent			
Cooperative			
Other:			

CHANGE-LEADERSHIP CHARACTERISTICS —ASSESSMENT BY OTHERS

Indicate the frequency with which _____ demonstrates the following critical change-leadership characteristics.

Characteristic	Rarely	Sometimes	Usually
Visionary			
Good listener			
Respects others			
Analytical			
Dependable			
Has a sense of humor			
Empathetic / caring			
Exhibits integrity			
Risk-taker			
Rewards/recognizes/ appreciates others			
Provides others with opportunities for growth			
Creative thinker			
Sets a good example / models desired behavior			
Inspiring			
Consistent			
Accountable			
Values diversity			
Servant to others			
Involves / engages others			
Fair			
Intelligent			
Cooperative			
Other:			

CHANGE-LEADERSHIP CHARACTERISTICS —ACTION PLAN FOR DEVELOPMENT

The following leadership plan is based upon self-reflection and feedback from my peers and employees.

Strengths: I do the following well, and will continue…

Developmental Areas: I need to improve the following …

The Plan: I will engage in the following specific actions to enhance my personal leadership skills and performance:

Action: Timeframe:

Action: Timeframe:

Action: Timeframe:

CHANGE-LEADERSHIP COMPETENCY QUESTIONNAIRE

I. VISIONARY	Rarely	Sometimes	Frequently	Always
Challenge the Status Quo				
1. I demonstrate willingness to take risks.	1	2	3	4
2. I possess thorough, in-depth knowledge of my industry, organization, and people.	1	2	3	4
3. Problem solving comes naturally to me.	1	2	3	4
4. I am consistently persuasive.	1	2	3	4
5. I am confident in my ability to lead others.	1	2	3	4
6. I adapt to ever-changing conditions.	1	2	3	4
7. I am results-driven.	1	2	3	4
8. I have a clear vision of my organization, including its potential and capabilities.	1	2	3	4
9. I am creative, able to envision that which does not yet exist.	1	2	3	4
10. I am comfortable with, not fearful of, ambiguity.	1	2	3	4
11. I demonstrate personal accountability for my decisions and actions.	1	2	3	4
12. I put the needs of others and my organization above my own.	1	2	3	4
13. I am long-term focused, resisting quick fix opportunities or short-term solutions.	1	2	3	4
14. I make certain that change initiatives support the organization's vision, mission, and goals.	1	2	3	4
15. I draw people in and build collaborative alliances of people working toward a common goal.	1	2	3	4
16. I willingly and enthusiastically share the organization's purpose and vision to ensure employee support.	1	2	3	4

Visionary Total Points _____

II. INSPIRER

	Rarely	Sometimes	Frequently	Always
17. I help people to see "what's in it for them" with regard to impending change.	1	2	3	4
18. I am unwaveringly enthusiastic about the benefits of change for individuals, groups, and the organization.	1	2	3	4
19. I allow employees to participate in the development of the organization's vision.	1	2	3	4
20. I work collaboratively *with* employees to accomplish the organization's goals and objectives.	1	2	3	4
21. I work with others to arrive at viable solutions.	1	2	3	4
22. I make certain that my values and beliefs align with those of the organization and the impending change.	1	2	3	4
23. I am the first to incorporate new ways and change into my daily routine.	1	2	3	4
24. My behaviors are consistent with my words.	1	2	3	4

Inspirer Total Points _____

III. SUPPORTER

	Rarely	Sometimes	Frequently	Always
25. I identify and eliminate barriers to change within my organization.	1	2	3	4
26. I allow employees to make mistakes and learn from their errors.	1	2	3	4
27. I am flexible, demonstrating my willingness to modify plans when necessary.	1	2	3	4
28. I am open to new ideas and fresh perspectives.	1	2	3	4
29. I encourage people to share their opinions, ideas, concerns, and suggestions for improvement.	1	2	3	4

(continued)

(continued)

30. I understand the intricacies of my organization, its players and capabilities, and use this knowledge to secure needed resources.	1	2	3	4
31. I am an advocate for my employees and pursue needed resources aggressively.	1	2	3	4
32. I encourage others to contribute and participate in ways that are meaningful to them.	1	2	3	4
33. I work with my employees as a coach rather than a boss.	1	2	3	4
34. I create a work environment free of fear.	1	2	3	4
35. I build trust by providing my employees the freedom to develop creative, innovative solutions to organizational challenges.	1	2	3	4
36. I continuously enhance my own written and verbal communications skills.	1	2	3	4
37. I develop a solid communication pattern with employees in terms of frequency and depth.	1	2	3	4
38. I devote my full attention to others and actively listen when I am being addressed.	1	2	3	4
39. I request feedback from my employees regarding my performance and behavior.	1	2	3	4
40. I visibly demonstrate my responsibility for change.	1	2	3	4
41. I hold myself accountable for the performance of my employees and the success of our projects.	1	2	3	4
42. I am honest and forthright with my intentions and actions.	1	2	3	4
43. My words are consistent with my actions and beliefs.	1	2	3	4
44. I demonstrate commitment to enhancing my skills by actively engaging in self development activities.	1	2	3	4

45. I engage in continual self reflection to develop an understanding of my own limitations.	1	2	3	4
46. I understand motivators of human behavior.	1	2	3	4
47. I personally get to know my employees and their unique talents, needs, goals, and wants.	1	2	3	4

Supporter Total Points_____

IV. PROBLEM SOLVER

	Rarely	Sometimes	Frequently	Always
48. I am able to employ multiple data gathering techniques, such as observation, surveys, interviews, and focus groups.	1	2	3	4
49. I am able to gather data, draw conclusions, propose and assess alternatives, and recommend viable solutions.	1	2	3	4
50. I think broadly to generate alternatives and engage in thorough analysis of viability.	1	2	3	4
51. I think "outside the box" and encourage the same in others.	1	2	3	4
52. I demonstrate resourcefulness in my approaches to new and existing problems or opportunities.	1	2	3	4
53. I become personally involved with employees, spending significant time with each in order to assess their skills, needs, and ways that I may be of assistance.	1	2	3	4
54. I work collaboratively with employees to evaluate the status of change efforts and modify as needed.	1	2	3	4

Problem Solver Total Points _____

(continued)

(continued)

V. CHANGE MANAGER	Rarely	Sometimes	Frequently	Always
55. I help employees work effectively and efficiently by minimizing organizational interference.	1	2	3	4
56. I understand the immense complexities of change, including planning, implementation, and human reactions.	1	2	3	4
57. I provide a communication climate that is non-threatening, comfortable, and conducive for sharing.	1	2	3	4
58. I openly communicate with employees to meet their needs and help them work through change.	1	2	3	4
59. I utilize a variety of methods to communicate, and tailor my delivery to the needs of my audience.	1	2	3	4
60. I understand the importance of goal setting and its relationship to employee motivation.	1	2	3	4
61. I work with employees to collaboratively set realistic, challenging, yet attainable goals and expectations.	1	2	3	4
62. I exhibit confidence in my employees' abilities and judgment.	1	2	3	4
63. I value the contributions of others and encourage their input.	1	2	3	4
64. I delegate work to others based on their skills, abilities, and interests.	1	2	3	4
65. I understand that resistance to change is natural yet can be overcome.	1	2	3	4
66. I take the time to discover the personal reactions and approaches to change unique to each employee.	1	2	3	4
67. I am familiar with and able to utilize specific techniques to help my employees work through change.	1	2	3	4

68. I understand that conflict can be constructive rather than destructive.	1	2	3	4
69. I am able to work with others to negotiate win-win solutions.	1	2	3	4
70. I know when to allow myself to become involved in employee conflict and when to function as an unbiased mediator.	1	2	3	4
71. I provide advancement and promotion opportunities for employees who embrace change.	1	2	3	4
72. I publicly recognize employees who promote and engage in change.	1	2	3	4
73. I reward employees (who change) in ways that are personally meaningful to them.	1	2	3	4
74. I link employees' adoption of change to appropriate recognition and rewards.	1	2	3	4
75. I engage employees in celebration of successful change efforts.	1	2	3	4

Change Manager
Total Points _____

SCORING THE CHANGE-LEADERSHIP QUESTIONNAIRE

After calculating the total for each of the five skill areas, total all five skill areas and compare this overall score to the Change-Leadership Competency Mastery Score line. An explanation of score ranges follows.

Visionary Total Points _____ (64)
Inspirer Total Points _____ (32)
Supporter Total Points _____ (92)
Problem Solver Total Points _____ (28)
Change Manager Total Points _____ (84)
Grand Total _____ (300)

ACTION PLAN FOR SELF-DEVELOPMENT

Review your competency areas, noting those areas of skill and those needing improvement. Plan to continue and further enhance your skill areas, as these clearly represent successes on your part.

Your lowest scores and related competencies offer areas for personal growth and development. Identify your weakest areas and formulate plans for enhancing your performance. List specific actions and appropriate timeframes for improvement. Action plans for your own personal development might include taking classes or attending workshops on change or leadership, seeking assistance from a mentor or successful change leader, asking your peers and employees for detailed feedback, and so forth. Visit this document regularly, and modify as needed to ensure your continued growth.

Change Leadership Competency Mastery Score

90	120	150	180	210	240	270	300
30%	40%	50%	60%	70%	80%	90%	100%

270+   **Change Leader**
You are an accomplished change leader. People recognize your talent and are comfortable following you through the journey of change. Continue to explore new ways to lead, encourage, involve, and reward.

240-269   **Change Agent**
You are a catalyst of change, are well on your way to being a leader, yet have room for improvement. Focus on perfecting your skills in developmental areas to enhance your effectiveness and the success of change efforts. Seek feedback from your peers and employees. In the end, you're all in this together.

210-239   **Average Change Manager**
Although you recognize the need for change, you struggle with certain critical components of the process, interactions with people, or your own roles and responsibilities. Be proactive. Assertively explore ways to hone your skills—include observation, workshops or courses, exploration of relevant literature, mentoring, and feedback.

<210   **Average Manager**
Like most managers, you have little if any training in implementing change, although you are required to do so. Change is probably as painful for you as it is for your employees. Now is the time to enhance your skills and effectiveness—embark on your own personal self development mission. You, your employees, and the organization will benefit.

CONCLUSION

The ability to assess one's skills, recognize strengths and weaknesses, and craft plans for personal growth and development is an indicator of true leadership. Change leaders understand that, for organizations to grow and develop, so must their employees at all levels. The tools in this chapter represent a small fraction of the instruments available to help individuals assess their skills and proactively plan ways to improve. Explore additional assessment instruments, for most provide valuable insight into who we are and how we can be more effective.

SIX

Tools for Success

If you want to truly understand something, try to change it.

—Kurt Lewin

Change is not a nice, neat, linear process. The steps of successful change in one organization at one point in time may not necessarily yield the same results for other, similar firms, or even the same organization under similar circumstances. Inputs vary—the leadership team experiences turnover, availability of resources declines, and so on. Successful change may follow multiple paths, which is why a variety of tools is offered next.

In this chapter you will find forms, worksheets, models, tips, and strategies to help you hone your skills as a change leader. These tools of the trade are designed to be used as they are or adapted to your own unique needs and situation.

Many of the tools require investigation on your part, followed by analysis and action planning. Information gathered from numerous sources (interviews, monthly/annual reports, other records) and employees at all levels of the firm will support the most accurate analysis. Although a vast amount of organizational knowledge resides with frontline employees, midlevel managers, and experienced personnel, relatively new hires can offer a fresh, less-biased perspective on organizational realities. In short, gather data from a wide variety of sources.

The tools offered in this chapter are as follows:

1. *Change Audit*—an assessment of an organization's past experiences with and present approach to change.
2. *SWOT Analysis*—assessment of the internal and external environments in which a firm operates; reveals internal strengths and weaknesses of a firm—its capabilities—as well as opportunities and threats posed by external factors.
3. *Steps in Analysis*—a systematic guide for conducting effective analyses of organizations, departments, or units.
4. *Barriers to Change*—a checklist of the common barriers to change within organizations.
5. *Plan for Conflict and Resistance*—a guide for anticipating and reacting to the conflict and resistance that occur as a result of change.
6. *Change Grid*—a tool for assessing individuals' current perceptions and approaches to impending change.
7. *Comprehensive Model for Change*—an in-depth guide to understanding, leading, and managing change.
8. *Create an Environment of Change*—compilation of the action steps necessary to build a culture of change.
9. *Strategic Communications Plan*—lists the common elements of communications planning and provides a guideline for use in planning communications related to change.
10. *Reward Strategies*—a checklist of the common monetary and nonmonetary rewards preferred by employees.
11. *Modify the Performance Management System*—guidelines for aligning a firm's performance management system (hiring practices, goal setting, coaching, appraisals, growth and development plans, and compensation/rewards) with desired change.
12. *Success Stories*—a brief compilation of true change "successes" shared by leaders and managers of change.

These tools are complementary. Each may be used as a stand-alone managerial aid in promoting change, or as a comprehensive set, depending on the complexity of the organization and your particular needs. Each instrument is preceded by a brief explanation. The specific tools are designed to be flexible; adapt them as needed to your organization.

Ideally, these tools will be most effective if employed prior to embarking on the journey of change. Proper planning sets the stage for effective implementation and prevents many problems before they occur.

The success stories are intended to provide you with examples of real approaches, including specific quotes and actions, utilized by a small group of change leaders. Although the approaches are varied, the results are not—successful change.

CHANGE AUDIT

Assessing an organization's ability to change is the first step in launching successful change initiatives. A change audit examines the history of change within the firm, the current state, and future capabilities. A historical perspective provides the foundation of analysis, while an examination of the current state frames the firm's present readiness for change and sets the stage for what must happen for change to be successful in the future.

This tool provides a framework for understanding an organization's propensity to change based on past experiences (e.g., the last 10 years, 20 years, and so forth) with change and current culture and capabilities. This tool is appropriate for use at the macro (organizational) and micro (division, department, or unit) levels within a firm.

The heart of an audit is investigation. You should survey executives, middle management, and frontline employees, both "lifers" and "new blood," to gather data about past change efforts, large or small, and their successes and failures. This tool should be expanded as necessary to reflect an organization's size and complexity.

Primary questions to answer include "who," "why," "when," "how," and "what." Who led the change and why? When did this occur? How was it implemented? What barriers were present? What were the results? This tool guides your efforts to identify gaps in the current versus desired state of change, along with plans for narrowing the gaps and working through and to change.

Change Audit

I. Historical Perspective of Change

In the past, what was the culture of the organization with respect to change (e.g., resistant, non-committal, aggressive, successful, inconsistent, etc.)?

What types of change have occurred?

- Small (changes in policy, procedures, etc)
- Moderate (new product, competitive challenges)
- Large-scale (merger, acquisition)

Specifically, describe the change initiatives:

Who was responsible for leading and implementing the change(s)?

Why was this particular person responsible?

When did the change effort occur?

How was the change implemented?

What were the barriers to change within the firm? (e.g., culture, poor management, lack of/poor communications, insufficient resources, etc.)

What were the results?

Define based on
- congruence with organizational goals, mission, and vision
- impact on people
- impact on processes / efficiency / service
- impact on profitability
- evidence that the changes were adopted and are now part of the daily workings of the firm

What would have been necessary for the change to have been (more) successful?

II. Current State of Readiness for Change

What is the current culture of the organization with respect to change (e.g., resistant, non-committal, aggressive, successful, inconsistent, etc.)?

Is the firm in the midst of any current change(s)? If so, describe: What types of change are occurring?

- Small (changes in policy, procedures, etc)

- Moderate (new product, competitive challenges)
- Large-scale (merger, acquisition)

Specifically, describe the change initiatives:

Who is responsible for leading and implementing the change(s)?

Why is this particular person responsible?

How is the change being implemented?

Describe the level of willingness of people to change.

- Do they recognize the need to change?
- What is the level of predisposition (or resistance) to change?

Describe the ability of people within the organization to change based on their

- knowledge of change
- change skills
- resilience

What barriers to change exist within the organization?

Typical barriers include
- policies, procedures
- organizational apathy or overconfidence
- dysfunctional culture
- poor leadership / management
- insufficient resources
- lack of rewards or consequences
- etc.

What will be necessary for the change to be successful?

III. Action Plan

What must happen for change to occur successfully? How can willingness be enhanced? How can the gaps in ability be lessened? How can barriers be reduced or eliminated?

Describe the desired outcome of the change. How will we measure results?

Define based on
- congruence with organizational goals, mission, and vision
- impact on people

- impact on processes / efficiency / service
- impact on profitability
- evidence that the changes were adopted and are now part of the daily workings of the firm

Who should lead the change(s) and why? Who else must be involved?

How should the change be implemented? What is the timeframe?

What resources are needed?

How can we overcome the barriers to change?

How should we celebrate our successes?

SWOT ANALYSIS

Analysis of the internal and external environments facing an organization or department enables its members to realistically plan for the future. SWOT stands for strengths, weaknesses, opportunities, and threats. Strengths and weaknesses reflect the internal environment and those conditions over which the organization has control. Strengths and weaknesses may include financial position and availability of resources; type of culture; talent of leaders, managers, and employees; effectiveness of policies and procedures; current market position; quality of product; reputation; loyalty of customers; and so forth.

Opportunities and threats are posed by the external environment and are largely beyond our scope of influence. Increasing competition, globalization, the legal and political environment, societal changes and trends, and natural disasters are a few examples.

Use this tool to honestly assess the position of your department, division, or organization with respect to impending change. Strengths and opportunities should be maximized, while weaknesses and threats are minimized. SWOT analysis also provides a guide for logically organizing "findings" useful in general analysis (tool #3).

SWOT Analysis

Unit/Department: **Date:**

Internal Environment		External Environment	
Strengths	Weaknesses	Opportunities	Threats

STEPS IN ANALYSIS

Analysis and problem solving are at the heart of change. The following guidelines offer a succinct means of information gathering and analysis, examination of alternatives, and making recommendations. Follow these steps whenever a project requires analysis of a situation and exploration of future steps:

1. Gather evidence, compile facts.
2. Draw conclusions as to the current state. Indicate the problem or opportunity.
3. Explore and analyze alternatives for solving the problem or maximizing the opportunity, or narrowing the gap between what is and what should be.
4. Recommend a viable solution(s) based on thorough examination of the alternative solutions.

PERFORMING THE STEPS

1. *Findings.* Gather the facts (verifiable information, data, statistics) surrounding the situation. Evidence in the form of quantifiable and qualifiable data will be housed in historical documents (company annual reports, department/division reports, human resource files) as well as with members of the organization (via observations, interviews, focus groups, and so forth). Bullet-point specific evidence for ease of reading.
2. *Problem or Opportunity.* Conclusions are drawn from the compilation of relevant evidence. "Based on our findings, a problem exists with...," or "the data indicate an opportunity lies with ..." Be careful to identify true causes of problems or opportunities, not merely symptoms.
3. *Alternatives.* Most problems or opportunities may be approached in a variety of ways. In this phase, brainstorm options and thoroughly assess the viability of each solution by determining the costs, benefits, pros, cons, timeframe, and overall reality of the particular solution. Include discussion of influence of corporate culture, leadership/ management and employee talent and capabilities, and any other factor that may affect the success of the alternative.
4. *Recommendation(s).* Recommendation(s) logically flow from the discussion of alternatives. Typically, the most viable alternative(s) proves to be the best, or most feasible, recommendation(s).

Sample Analysis

Findings:

- Account management relies on a decades-old, manual system of recording client information.
- Field representatives manually record the details of account calls and submit weekly reports to the home office.
- Receipt of weekly reports is sporadic due to remote locations of some representatives, unreliability of mail system, and lack of perceived importance.
- Competitors utilize laptop computers for presentations with accounts and to report client information.
- Clients have reported that competitors offer more sophisticated, higher quality presentations.
- Clients have reported sending their business to competitors due to perceptions of higher quality and faster service.
- Field representatives are resistant to automation; fears of "big brother"
- Etc.

Problem/Opportunity:

Our antiquated account management system inhibits the competitiveness of our sales force and is negatively impacting sales.

Alternatives:

1. no change
   - Unacceptable. We are currently losing business; the situation will worsen.
2. utilize a vendor-supplied system of account management
   - pro: expertise readily available; implementation within a month
   - con: cost of hardware, software, and training - $55,000; not specific to our firm, products, sales force, or clients; resistance of sales force.
3. contract with vendor to customize an account management system for our sales force
   - pro: specifically meets the needs of our firm, products, sales force, clients; relatively rapid development and implementation – estimate of 3 months
   - con: higher cost for customized system – bid of $82,000; expensive to modify; resistance of sales force.
4. develop our own customized system to manage account information
   - pro: specifically meets the needs of our firm, personnel, and clients; we own and may modify at any time
   - con: limited talent and resources in-house to design, implement, monitor, and modify; no experience in developing software of this sort; resistance of sales force.

Recommendation(s):

We must automate our field sales force in order to maintain or improve our position in the marketplace. Due to limited in-house capabilities, resources, and time, Option 3 is most feasible.

IDENTIFYING BARRIERS TO CHANGE

This is a list of some of the most common barriers to change within organizations. Assess your organization—look for barriers at all levels, in all places. Difficulties with change will be present. When you locate a barrier, look for the cause or source. This may be a poor policy or procedure, element of culture, or a member of management, to name a few. To reduce the barrier, you must address or overcome the cause.

Overcoming barriers to change requires specific actions or strategies. Identify "who" will be responsible for "what" and "when." Involve employees in the discussion of barriers, causes, and strategies for resolution. Assign specific duties based on agreement of skill, interest, and available time for engagement.

Identify and Overcome Barriers to Change

Barrier	Cause / Source	Strategy to Overcome
Lack of information about the change		
Organizational apathy or overconfidence		
Dysfunctional culture		
Lack of leadership for the change		
Insufficient allocation of resources to the change		
Lack of management support for the change		
Policies or procedures that hinder the change: list specifically		
Lack of rewards or consequences for change		
Other		

PLAN FOR CONFLICT AND RESISTANCE

Change produces conflict; it is inevitable. Similarly, resistance will surface. Use this checklist as a tool to help develop an approach to minimize conflict and resistance before they occur, and deal with these obstacles once they surface.

Keep in mind that you are not in this alone. You *and* your employees will resist efforts at change or engage in conflict. Involve others in this discussion—tap their intelligence, ideas, and talent.

☐ Understand that conflict and resistance will occur—these are natural human responses to change.

☐ Make no assumptions that "everyone is on board." Still waters run deep.

☐ Recognize that conflict can be healthy—it is not always negative.

☐ Know that resistance is a symptom of an underlying root cause; it provides an opportunity to bring problems or barriers to the surface, where they may be addressed and overcome.

☐ Involve others in developing solutions to conflict and resistance.

☐ Discuss the potential for conflict or resistance with those who will be impacted by the change; ask

• How will this change impact you?
• What conflict(s) do you think will occur?
• How can we resolve the conflict?
• What will you as an individual need to work through this change?

☐ Plan to share information in a timely, substantive fashion. Resistance is often the result of insufficient information or misunderstandings regarding the impending change.

☐ Communicate in ways that meet individuals' needs (e.g., face-to-face, in writing, via e-mail, etc.).

☐ Treat people and their issues as unique. Change, resistance, and conflict are very personal.

☐ Share your own feelings and strategies for overcoming your own resistance or conflicts.

☐ Encourage others to resolve their own interpersonal conflicts.

☐ Know when to intervene in others' conflicts and when to back off.

☐ Help create win-win situations, that is, benefits for all parties.

☐ Reward individuals and groups for successfully resolving conflicts or overcoming resistance.

THE CHANGE GRID

Understanding human reactions to change helps organizations plan for the change, communicate, and guide individuals through the process. The change grid (Figure 2.2 from chapter 2) visually depicts individuals' current reactions to change. Helping individuals work through the various phases of change requires understanding their present perceptions and behaviors, and meeting their needs with respect to the impending change.

To use this tool, first identify the words and behaviors that reveal individuals' emotions and their location on the grid. Next, initiate strategies to help people work through their issues and toward exploration and commitment. Remember, communication and involvement are critical.

1. Evaluate individuals' words and behaviors.
2. Plot locations of individuals on the grid.
3. Identify individual-specific strategies for working toward change.

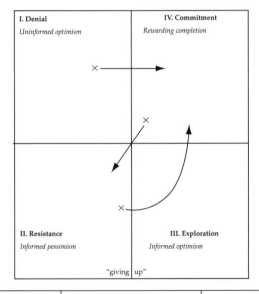

Who is impacted by the impending change?	Where is he/she with respect to change?	How to help him/her/them move forward?

COMPREHENSIVE MODEL FOR CHANGE

This is a list of the steps in the change process. It provides a guide for implementing change as well as preparing for the inevitable conflict and resistance that will occur. Involve those who will be impacted by the change from the outset. Share this list and collaboratively create an action plan for success.

Comprehensive Model for Change

	1. recognize that change is immensely complex; nonlinear
	2. understand individual and organizational responses (resistance) to change, and how to deal with these responses
	3. create a culture that supports change
	4. establish a vision for change
	5. build a guiding coalition for the change
	6. "sell" the change to all levels of the organization; help individuals understand that the change is necessary, urgent; teach that change is good, desirable
	7. remove barriers to action
	8. involve employees at all levels in the change process (including planning, implementation, monitoring, and rewarding)
	9. communicate proficiently; solicit input and share information with those impacted by the change
	10. prepare for and plan responses to resistance; treat resistance to change as an opportunity; understand that resistance is a symptom of a deeper problem (e.g., poor management or strategy, ineffective communication, etc.)
	11. deal with employees and their reactions individually, not as a group
	12. execute the change in small increments
	13. constantly monitor progress of the change initiative and refine/adjust as needed
	14. reward individuals and groups for engaging in change
	15. celebrate short- and long-term wins
	16. solidify the change in the newly emerged culture

CREATE AN ENVIRONMENT OF CHANGE

Creating a culture of change is a lengthy process—culture tends to evolve slowly over time. Much of successful change depends on relationships, collaboration, and trust. Trust takes a long time to develop, yet can be destroyed in a matter of seconds. Creating an environment that supports change requires dedication and commitment, often in light of pressure for immediate results.

Use these guidelines to create an environment of change. Discuss them with your staff and secure their ideas. For each, work collaboratively with your staff and peers to craft and engage in strategies for success.

Create an Environment of Change

Action	*How?*
Hire individuals with a predisposition to change and high tolerance for ambiguity.	
Enhance your own change skills.	
Encourage and reward innovation, creativity, and risk-taking.	
Do not micromanage; be a resource, coach, partner, and guide.	
Identify and remove barriers to change.	
Fight for resources.	
Allow failure and encourage people to learn from their mistakes.	
Trust your people – and make certain they know it.	
Involve people at all levels in change.	
Engage in change frequently and incrementally.	
Promote the benefits of change and help people to see change as an opportunity.	
Help individuals assess how change will benefit them personally.	
Encourage people to work through change together.	
Provide forums for discussion; actively seek and act on feedback.	
Celebrate small victories and milestones.	
Reward those who change, both individually and in groups.	
Other:	

STRATEGIC COMMUNICATIONS PLAN

Communications is an often-ignored aspect of strategy, particularly with respect to change. This list of common elements of planning communications addresses who needs to know what, when, and how. This tool is useful in planning large- and small-scale communications in a variety of settings, such as new product introductions, upcoming changes in benefits, or a new system implementation, to name a few.

1. Map the communications strategy.
   - Identify the target audience—who needs to know (e.g., shareholders, customers, community, vendors, employees—at what levels)?
   - What specific information should be shared?
   - How should the information be shared—by what method?
     Individually, face-to-face
     Group meeting
     Personal phone call
     Formal letter
     Company memorandum
     E-mail
     Personal
     Group, department, or division
     Company-wide
     Press release
     Other
   - When is the information necessary—pre-event, during the event, or post-event?
2. Create a detailed communications timeline.
3. Hold people accountable.

Communications Plan for:

Audience	Specific Information to be Shared	Method or Media	Timeframe / Date(s)

REWARD STRATEGIES

Like change, motivators and rewards are very personal. Involve others—ask them what rewards will be appropriate and what will motivate them to change. No one-size-fits-all strategy will work—what is meaningful to one person may be insignificant to another.

This checklist highlights some of the most common monetary and non-monetary rewards listed as meaningful by employees in recent surveys (employees typically rank cash no higher than fourth). This list is by no means all-inclusive. Work with your staff to develop rewards suitable to the change and their efforts.

Monetary and Non-Monetary Rewards

Monetary rewards	Non-monetary rewards
☐ individual bonuses	☐ appreciation ("thank you")
☐ group bonuses	☐ interesting work; challenge
☐ gift certificates	☐ vacation, leisure time
☐ company stock	☐ responsibility and authority
☐ company product(s) or discounts	☐ recognition certificates or plaques
☐ % of cost savings for new ideas	☐ flexible work schedule
☐ gift for children or spouse	☐ freedom and independence
☐ individual or group lunches	☐ fun
	☐ special privileges

MODIFY THE PERFORMANCE MANAGEMENT SYSTEM

Organizations share the seriousness of change by incorporating change competencies into all aspects of the performance management (PM) system. This tool provides guidelines for including change terminology, competencies, and expectations into daily routines as guided by the PM system. The components of a successful PM system are

1. hiring
2. establishing goals, standards, and expectations
3. coaching and training
4. developmental evaluations
5. growth and development plans
6. compensation and rewards

1. Hire People Who Are Prepared to Change
- ❑ seek individuals with a predisposition to change; this may include a high tolerance of ambiguity and stress
- ❑ include change competencies in job descriptions and job postings

Sample Interview Questions

Explain your approach to change.
How do you react to change?
Describe a time when you were required to change and how you coped.
How do you handle stress?

Sample Position Descriptors

Must thrive in a fast-paced, constantly changing environment.
High tolerance of ambiguity.
Able to manage highly stressful projects.

2. Establish Goals, Standards, and Expectations
- ❑ discuss goals, standards, and expectations *prior* to engaging in change
- ❑ incorporate change into all individual, unit, and department goals and expectations
- ❑ include specific change skills to be enhanced

3. Coach and Train
- ❑ model/live the change
- ❑ give feedback to others regarding their efforts

❏ help others perfect their change skills by providing education, training, and opportunities to practice

4. Developmental Evaluations
❏ hold people accountable for change
❏ include requirements for change in regular performance appraisals—whether formal or informal

5. Growth and Development Plans
❏ include change criteria and skills in plans for future individual growth and development
❏ identify resources and support needed for growth and development of change competencies

6. Compensation and Rewards
❏ identify specific motivators needed by individuals to help them engage in change
❏ reward individuals and groups for their change efforts

SUCCESS STORIES

Sometimes the greatest managerial tool is simply an understanding of people. The following true stories and anecdotes provide examples of various techniques used by leaders and managers to promote change. All stem from developing effective relationships with employees, understanding their needs and concerns, and taking the time to plan rather than react. Individual names and organizations have been withheld at the request of the majority of those involved.

If you have any stories of change (successful or not) you would like to share, please contact me at gilleya@ferris.edu.

1. Realizing that his division consisted of a very diverse group of people, the regional manager asked, "What do you need to make this change work? What must happen for you to embrace it?"
2. The vice president of agency management held a weekly department meeting in which members shared challenges, successes, and feedback regarding the previous week. She also met with each member of the department individually each month to discuss successes, challenges, goals, opportunities for improvement, and so forth. She exhibited an open-door policy that encouraged interaction and feedback from individuals at all levels.
3. Employees of a relatively small company that had downsized from 11 to 7 needed new ways to approach their work tasks. They could

no longer afford very specialized job titles and responsibilities. They were all in this together. The owner prioritized tasks to be accomplished each day, and often placed the most rewarding tasks at the top of the list. As employees arrived at work, they chose which projects to work on each day—first come, first choice of projects. As an individual completed his or her task, another from the list was chosen until all (or most) had been completed by the end of the day.

4. As the manager of a 400-account territory, I depended on the stability of my company and the quality of our products for my livelihood. The discontinuation of a popular (insurance) product caused a great deal of initial pain for my accounts and, thus, for me. However, the product was losing money for the company. The home office shared key data regarding the product, losses, and profitability. Absent this particular product, our loss ratios and profitability would improve, which meant higher bonuses for my accounts and me. Although a painful short-term financial loss for me and my accounts, the long-term benefits were clear. This I communicated to my accounts.

5. Field sales representatives were told they would soon have laptop computers. Initially, they reacted with fear and resentment—big brother would be watching! Eventually, however, they were sold. They would be better able to compete with competitors by offering clients PowerPoint presentations and design services in their offices. More business meant goals would be met, bonuses would be bigger, and promotional opportunities would follow.

6. In the face of impending change, the department manager gathered his people together and stated, "We can manage this change or be victims of it—but it will happen." Together, they honestly discussed the change, its potential impacts, and their involvement.

7. Employees at a large bank are encouraged to expand their knowledge and abilities. After attending workshops or seminars, individuals first discuss their learning with their managers to identify opportunities for improvement in the workplace. Attendees then present their ideas to the larger group, and the group brainstorms ways to implement the positives.

8. When the corporate communications director of a major university recognized the need for a new performance-appraisal system, she contacted a consultant to lead the process. All employees were asked to participate and provide input. Then the consultant guided employees through a series of iterations in which they developed their own performance-appraisal system—vastly different from the original.

9. The president of a regional firm spoke to all employees every quarter (in company-wide meetings that typically lasted about an hour) to keep them updated on the state of the company. He shared financial information, new product initiatives, and legislative changes. Although the meetings were mandatory, employees were rewarded for attendance with door prizes, gift certificates, and up-to-date information on the firm.

10. A large company (1,000 employees) moved to a new corporate headquarters building. The move was completed in waves, over two weeks, to lessen chaos and provide individuals with sufficient time to acclimate to their new surroundings.

11. A certain vice president keeps her office well supplied with critical munchies—pretzels, chips, sweets and such—that she shares. These snacks bring people from all levels of the organization—from executive vice president to administrative assistant—to her door. The result? She's in the loop, and people from different areas make valuable connections with each other.

12. Each month, members of a 15-person marketing division who have engaged in change are rewarded for their efforts with small ($5–$10) gift certificates to local restaurants. Individuals must be nominated by their peers. The department also has a traveling "go the extra mile" award—a St. Bernard figure—presented to one member of the group who has exhibited behavior above and beyond the call of duty sometime during the previous week. This award, which also requires nomination by one's peers, is proudly displayed on desks and in offices until the next meeting.

13. After reorganization of the department, job redesign, and development of new job descriptions, members of the department, in conjunction with a representative from human resources, created a new 360-degree performance appraisal form that incorporated change into its requirements.

CONCLUSION

Organizations and their members must continually change to survive. Fortunately, change leaders have quite a few tools at their disposal. Armed with the tools in this chapter (in their present form or some modification), their personal insight into change, and the support and involvement of their peers and staff, champions of change can chart a course for success.

SEVEN

Resources for the Manager as Change Leader

We can change our whole life and the attitude of people around us simply by changing ourselves.

—Rudolph Dreidurs

The resources in this chapter are designed for action-oriented change leaders who like concise, readily available information. An enormous amount of information exists on the topic of change. As a result, the following list of resources is by no mean all-inclusive. A complete list would be a book in and of itself. The books, journals, articles, and organizations listed will, however, provide a solid foundation.

The list of books and articles includes all of the books referenced in each chapter, along with other related works you may find valuable. The journals address issues related to human performance within organizations. The journals list contains a combination of resources, from works based on quantitative and qualitative research to theoretical explorations of ideas or topics. Finally, the organizations are devoted to improving performance—which requires change—within organizations.

BOOKS

Abrahamson, Eric. *Change without Pain*. Boston: Harvard Business School Press, 2003.

Anderson, Dean, and Linda A. Anderson. *Beyond Change Management: Advanced Strategies for Today's Transformational Leaders*. San Francisco: Jossey-Bass/Pfeiffer, 2001.

Argyris, Chris. *Knowledge for Action: A Guide to Overcoming Barriers to Organizational Change*. San Francisco: Jossey-Bass, 1993.

Auger, M. J., and J. A. Ross. "The Biology of the Macrophage." In *The Macrophage*, edited by C. E. Lewis and J. O'D. McGee, pp. 1–12. Oxford: Oxford University Press, 1992.

Axelrod, Richard H. *Terms of Engagement: Changing the Way We Change Organizations*. San Francisco: Berrett-Koehler, 2002.

Bateman, Thomas S., and Scott A. Snell. *Management: Building Competitive Advantage*. 4th ed. Boston: Irwin McGraw-Hill, 1999.

Beer, Michael, and Nitin Nohria. *Breaking the Code of Change*. Boston: Harvard Business School Press, 2000.

Block, Peter. *Stewardship*. San Francisco: Berrett-Koehler Publishers, 1992.

Bolman, Lee G. and Terrence E. Deal. Reframing Organizations: Artistry, Choice, and Leadership. 3rd ed. San Francisco: Jossey-Bass, 2003.

Buckingham, Marcus, and Donald O. Clifton. *Now, Discover Your Strengths*. New York: The Free Press, 2001.

Collins, Jim. *Good to Great: Why Some Companies Make the Leap...and Others Don't*. New York: Harper Business, 2001.

Conner, D. *Managing at the Speed of Change*. New York: Villard Books, 1992.

Drucker, Peter F. *Managing in a Time of Great Change*. New York: Truman Talley Books/Dutton, 1995.

Galpin, Timothy J. *The Human Side of Change*. San Francisco: Jossey-Bass, 1996.

Gilley, Jerry W., and Nathaniel W. Boughton. *Stop Managing, Start Coaching!* Chicago: Irwin Professional Publishing, 1996.

Gilley, Jerry W., and Ann Gilley. *Organizational Learning, Performance, and Change: An Introduction to Strategic HRD*. Cambridge, MA: Perseus Publishing, 2000.

———. *Strategically Integrated HRD: Six Transformational Roles in Creating Results-Driven Programs*. 2nd ed. Cambridge, MA: Perseus Publishing, 2003.

Gilley, Jerry W., Scott A. Quatro, Erik Hoekstra, Doug Whittle, and Ann Maycunich. *The Manager as Change Agent*. Cambridge, MA: Perseus Publishing, 2001.

Goldsby, R. A., T. J. Kindt, and B. A. Osborne. "Overview of the Immune System." In *Immunology*, edited by J. Kuby, pp. 3–26. New York: W. H. Freeman, 2000.

Habeck, M. M., F. Kroger, and M. R. Tram. *After the Merger: Seven Rules for Successful Post-merger Integration*. Harlow, England: Financial Times/Prentice Hall, 2000.

Harless, Joe H. *An Ounce of Analysis (Is Worth a Pound of Objectives)*. Newnan, GA: Harless Press, 1980.

Ivancevich, John M., and Michael T. Matteson. *Organizational Behavior and Management*. 5th ed. Boston: Irwin McGraw-Hill, 1999.

Judson, A. S. *Changing Behavior in Organizations: Minimizing Resistance to Change*. Cambridge, MA: Blackwell, 1991.

Katz, D., and R. L. Kahn. *The Social Psychology of Organizations*. 2nd ed. New York: Wiley and Sons, 1978.

Katzenbach, J. R. *Real Change Leaders*. New York: Random House, 1995.

Kissler, G. D. *The Change Riders: Managing the Power of Change*. Reading, MA: Addison-Wesley Publishing Company, 1991.

Kotter, John P. *Leading Change*. Boston: Harvard Business School Press, 1996.

Kotter, John P., and D. S. Cohen. *The Heart of Change: Real-Life Stories of How People Change Their Organizations*. Boston, MA: Harvard Business School Press, 2002.

Kouzes, James M., and Barry M. Posner. *The Leadership Challenge*. San Francisco: Jossey-Bass, 1995.

Kreitner, Robert, and Angelo Kinicki. *Organizational Behavior*. New York: Irwin McGraw-Hill, 2004.

Kuby, J. *Immunology*. New York: W. H. Freeman and Co., 2000.

Lewin, Kurt. *Field Theory in Social Science*. New York: Harper, 1951.

Malcolm Baldridge National Quality Award. *Criteria for Performance Excellence*. Washington, DC: U.S. Department of Commerce, 1998.

Maslow, Abraham H. *Motivation and Personality*. New York: Harper & Row, 1987.

McLagan, R., and C. Nel. *The Age of Participation*. San Francisco: Berrett-Koehler, 1995.

Mercer, Michael W. *Absolutely Fabulous Organizational Change: Strategies for Success from America's Best-Run Companies*. New York: AMACOM, 2000.

Moss Kanter, R. *The Change Masters*. New York: Simon & Schuster, 1983.

Nadler, David A. *Champions of Change: How CEOs and Their Companies Are Mastering the Skills of Radical Change*. San Francisco: Jossey-Bass Publishers, 1998.

Newell, Alan, and Herbert A. Simon. *Human Problem Solving*. Englewood Cliffs, NJ: Prentice Hall, 1972.

Pacsale, Richard T., Mark Millemann, and Linda Gioja. *Surfing the Edge of Chaos: The Laws of Nature and the New Laws of Business.* New York: Crown Business, 2000.

Patterson, J. *Coming Clean about Organizational Change.* Arlington, VA: American Association of School Administrators, 1997.

Peterson, D. B., and M. D. Hicks. *Leader as Coach: Strategies for Coaching and Developing Others.* Minneapolis, MN: Personnel Decisions International, 1996.

Pfeiffer, Jeffrey. *Competitive Advantage through People.* Boston: Harvard Business School Press, 1994.

The Price Waterhouse Change Integration Team. *The Paradox Principles: How High-Performance Companies Manage Chaos, Complexity, and Contradiction to Achieve Superior Results.* Chicago: Irwin Professional Publishing, 1996.

Ratner, B. D., A. S. Hoffman, F. J. Schoen, and J. E. Lemons, eds. *Biomaterials Science: An Introduction to Materials in Medicine.* San Diego: Academic Press, 1996.

Rogers, Everett M. *Diffusion of Innovations.* 4th ed. New York: The Free Press, 1995.

Rummler, Geary A., and Alan P. Brache. *Improving Performance: How to Manage the White Space on the Organizational Chart.* San Francisco: Jossey-Bass, 1990.

Selye, H. *Stress without Distress.* New York: J B Lippincott, 1974.

Senge, Peter. *The Fifth Disciple: The Art and Practice of the Learning Organization.* New York: Doubleday/Currency, 1990.

Senn, Larry. "Culture." In *The Arthur Young Management Guide to Mergers and Acquisitions,* edited by R. S. Bibler, pp. 229–243. New York: John Wiley & Sons, 1989.

Tjosvold, D. *Learning to Manage Conflict: Getting People to Work Together Productively.* New York: Lexington Books, 1993.

Ulrich, David. *Human Resource Champions.* Boston: Harvard Business School Press, 1998.

Weisbord, M. R. *Productive Workplaces: Organizing and Managing for Dignity, Meaning, and Community.* San Francisco: Jossey-Bass, 1987.

Wheatley, Margaret J. *Leadership and the New Science: Learning about Organizations from an Orderly Universe.* San Francisco: Berrett-Koehler, 1992.

ARTICLES

Allen, Stephen A. "Organizational Choice and General Influence Networks for Diversified Companies." *Academy of Management Journal* (September 1978): p. 341.

Beer, M., R.A. Eisenstat, and B. Spector. "Why Change Programs Don't Produce Change." *Harvard Business Review,* November/December 1990, pp. 158–166.

Bovey, W.H., and A. Hede. "Resistance to Organizational Change: The Role of Defense Mechanisms." *Journal of Managerial Psychology* 16, no. 7 (2001): pp. 534–549.

Coghlan, D. "A Person-Centered Approach to Dealing with Resistance to Change." *Leadership and Organizational Development Journal* 14, no. 4 (1993): pp. 10–14.

Doyle, M. "Change Management—or Change Leadership?" *Human Resource Management Journal* 12, no. 1 (2002): pp. 3–17.

Doyle, M. "Selecting Managers for Transformational Change." *Human Resource Management Journal* 12, no. 1 (2002): pp. 3–17.

Keagan, R., and L.L. Lahey. "The Real Reason People Won't Change." *Harvard Business Review,* November, 2001, p. 84.

Kotter, John P. "Leading Change: Why Transformation Efforts Fail." *Harvard Business Review,* March/April 1995, pp. 59–67.

Kotter, John P., and L.A. Schlesinger. "Choosing Strategies for Change." *Harvard Business Review,* March/April 1979, pp. 106–114.

Lawrence, P.R. "How to Deal with Resistance to Change." *Harvard Business Review,* May/June 1954, pp. 49–57.

Morrow, I.J. "Making Change Irresistible: Overcoming Resistance to Change in Your Organization." *Personnel Psychology* 52, no. 3 (1999): 816–820.

Nadler, D.A. "Managing Organizational Change: An Integrative Perspective." *Journal of Applied Behavioral Science* 17, no. 2 (1981): pp. 191–211.

Pacsale, Richard T., Mark Millemann, and Linda Gioja. "Changing the Way We Change." *Harvard Business Review,* November/December 1997, p. 126.

Scott, C.D., and D.T. Jaffe. "Survive and Thrive in Times of Change." *Training and Development Journal* 42, no. 4 (1988): pp. 25–27.

Strebel, P. "Why Do Employees Resist Change?" *Harvard Business Review,* May/June 1996, pp. 86–92.

Trader-Leigh, K.E. "Identifying Resistance in Managing Change." *Journal of Organizational Change Management* 15, no. 2 (2002): pp. 138–156.

Wall Jr., J.A., and R.R. Callister. "Conflict and Its Management." *Journal of Management* 3 (1995): p. 517.

Webber, A.M. "Learning for a Change." *Fast Company,* May 1999, p. 180.

Zaleznik, A. "The Leadership Gap." *The Executive* 4 (February 1990): pp. 7–22.

Zander, A.F. "Resistance to Change—Its Analysis and Prevention." *Advanced Management* 1, no. 5 (1950): pp. 9–11.

JOURNALS

Academy of Management Executives
www.aomonline.org (click on Publications)
Academy of Management Journal
www.aomonline.org
Academy of Management Review
www.aomonline.org
Administrative Science Quarterly
www.johnson.cornell.edu/publications/asq
Advanced Management
www.cob.tamucc.edu/sam/amj
Group and Organization Management
www.sagepub.com (click on Journals)
Harvard Business Review
www.harvardbusinessonline.hbsp.harvard.edu
Human Resource Development Quarterly
www.hrdq.com
Human Resource Development Review
www.sagepub.com (click on Journals; Business and Management)
Human Resource Management Review
www.elsevier.com (click on Journals)
International Journal of Conflict Management
www.members.aol.com/mgt2000/ijcm.htm
International Journal of Human Resource Management
www.tandf.co.uk/journals
Journal of Applied Behavioral Science
www.sagepub.com (click on Business and Management)
Journal of Business Strategy
www.managementfirst.com (click on Strategy, then Journals)
Journal of Change Management
www.tandf.co.uk/journals/titles/14697017.asp
Journal of Human Resources
www.ssc.wisc.edu/jhr
Journal of Management
www.sagepub.com (click on Business and Management)
www.elsevier.com
Journal of Management Development
www.managementfirst.com (click on Public Sector, then Journals)
Journal of Management Studies
www.blackwellpublishing.com (click on Journals)
Journal of Managerial Issues
www.pittstate.edu/econ/jmi.html

Journal of Managerial Psychology
www.managementfirst.com (click on Public Sector, then Journals)
Journal of Organizational Behavior
www.wiley.com (click on Business; General Business; Journals)
Journal of Organizational Behavior Management
www.haworthpressinc.com/web/JOBM
Journal of Organizational Change Management
www.managementfirst.com (click on Change Management, then Journals)
Journal of Organizational Excellence
www.wiley.com (click on Business; General Business; Journals)
Leadership and Organizational Development Journal
www.managementfirst.com (click on HR, then Journals)
Organizational Behavior and Human Decision Processes
www.elsevier.com (click on Journals)
Performance Improvement Quarterly
www.ispi.org/publications/piq
Personnel Psychology
www.blackwell-synergy.com (click on List of Journals)
Training
www.trainingmag.com

ORGANIZATIONS

Academy of Human Resource Development
AHRD, College of Technology
Bowling Green State University
Bowling Green, OH 43403-0301
419-372-9155
Fax 419-372-8385
www.ahrd.org

Academy of Management
235 Elm Rd.
P.O. Box 3020
Briarcliff Manor, NY 10510-8020
914-923-2607
Fax 914-923-2615
www.aomonline.org

American Management Association
1601 Broadway
New York, NY 10019
212-586-8100 or 800-262-9699

Fax 212-903-8168
www.amanet.org

American Society for Training and Development
1640 King St.
Box 1443
Alexandria, VA 22313-2043
704-683-8100
Fax 704-683-8103
www.astd.org

International Society for Performance Improvement
1400 Spring St., Suite 260
Silver Spring, MD 20910
301-587-8570
Fax 301-587-8573
www.ispi.org

Society for Human Resource Management
1800 Duke St.
Alexandria, VA 22314
800-283-SHRM
Fax 703-535-6490
www.shrm.org

Notes

CHAPTER 1

1. Michael Beer and Nitin Nohria, *Breaking the Code of Change* (Boston: Harvard Business School Press, 2000).

2. Study by J. I. Porras and P. J. Robertson, 1983.

3. M. Beer, R. A. Eisenstat, and B. Spector, "Why Change Programs Don't Produce Change," *Harvard Business Review,* November/December 1990, pp. 158–166.

4. P. Strebel, "Why Do Employees Resist Change?" *Harvard Business Review,* May/June 1996, pp. 86–92.

5. Stephen A. Allen, "Organizational Choice and General Influence Networks for Diversified Companies," *Academy of Management Journal* (September 1978): p. 341.

6. David A. Nadler, *Champions of Change: How CEOs and Their Companies Are Mastering the Skills of Radical Change* (San Francisco: Jossey-Bass Publishers, 1998), p. 11.

7. Beer, Eisenstat, and Spector, "Why Change Programs Don't Produce Change," pp. 158–166; R. S. Bibler, *The Arthur Young Management Guide to Mergers and Acquisitions* (New York: John Wiley & Sons, 1989); J. I. Porras

and P.J. Robertson, "Organization Development: Theory, Practice, and Research," in *The Handbook of Industrial and Organizational Psychology*, vol. 3., ed. M.D. Dunnette and L.M. Hough (Palo Alto, CA: Consulting Psychologists Press, 1983), pp. 719–822.

8. Robert Kreitner and Angelo Kinicki, *Organizational Behavior* (New York: Irwin McGraw-Hill, 2004), p. 118.

9. John M. Ivancevich and Michael T. Matteson, *Organizational Behavior and Management*, 5th ed. (Boston: Irwin McGraw-Hill, 1999); Thomas S. Bateman and Scott A. Snell, *Management: Building Competitive Advantage*, 4th ed. (Boston: Irwin McGraw-Hill, 1999).

10. David Ulrich, *Human Resource Champions* (Boston: Harvard Business School Press, 1998), p. 157.

11. Nadler, *Champions of Change*, p. 3.

CHAPTER 2

1. David A. Nadler, *Champions of Change: How CEOs and Their Companies Are Mastering the Skills of Radical Change* (San Francisco: Jossey-Bass Publishers, 1998), pp. 14–15.

2. D. Conner, *Managing at the Speed of Change* (New York: Villard Books, 1992).

3. Everett M. Rogers, *Diffusion of Innovations*, 4th ed. (New York: The Free Press, 1995).

4. Ibid., pp. 272–274.

5. C.D. Scott and D.T. Jaffe, "Survive and Thrive in Times of Change," *Training and Development Journal* (April 1988): pp. 25–27.

6. Larry Senn, "Culture," in *The Arthur Young Management Guide to Mergers and Acquisitions*, ed. R.S. Bibler (New York: John Wiley & Sons, 1989), pp. 229–243.

7. M.M. Habeck, F. Kroger, and M.R. Tram, *After the Merger: Seven Rules for Successful Post-merger Integration* (Harlow, England: Financial Times/ Prentice Hall, 2000).

8. Jerry W. Gilley and Ann Gilley, *Strategically Integrated HRD: Six Transformational Roles in Creating Results-Driven Programs*, 2nd ed. (Cambridge, MA: Perseus Publishing, 2003).

9. R.A. Goldsby, T.J. Kindt, and B.A. Osborne, "Overview of the Immune System," in *Immunology*, ed. J. Kuby (New York: W.H. Freeman, 2000), pp. 3–26; D.P. Speert, "Macrophages in Bacterial Infection," in *The Macrophage*, ed. C.E. Lewis and J.O'D. McGee (Oxford: Oxford University Press, 1992), pp. 217–263.

10. R. A. Goldsby, T. J. Kindt, and B. A. Osborne, "Transplant Immunity," in *Immunology,* ed. J. Kuby (New York: W. H. Freeman, 2000), pp. 517–538.

11. M. J. Auger and J. A. Ross, "The Biology of the Macrophage," in *The Macrophage,* ed. C. E. Lewis and J.O'D. McGee (Oxford: Oxford University Press, 1992), pp. 1–12.

12. J. M. Anderson, A. G. Gristina, S. R. Hanson, L. A. Harker, R. J. Johnson, K. Merritt, P. T. Taylor, and F. J. Schoen, "Host Reactions to Biomaterials and Their Evaluation," in *Biomaterials Science: An Introduction to Materials in Medicine,* ed. B. D. Ratner, A. S. Hoffman, F. J. Schoen, and J. E. Lemons (San Diego: Academic Press, 1996), pp. 165–214.

13. R. A. Goldsby, T. J. Kindt, and B. A. Osborne, "Leukocyte Migration and Inflammation," in *Immunology,* ed. J. Kuby (New York: W. H. Freeman, 2000), pp. 384–385.

14. Ibid.; F. A. Davis, *Taber's Cyclopedic Medical Dictionary,* 16th ed. (Philadelphia: F. A. Davis, 1989).

15. Davis, *Taber's Cyclopedic Medical Dictionary*; R. A. Goldsby, T. J. Kindt, and B. A. Osborne, "Cancer and the Immune System," in *Immunology,* ed. J. Kuby (New York: W. H. Freeman, 2000), pp. 539–540.

16. A. S. Judson, *Changing Behavior in Organizations: Minimizing Resistance to Change* (Cambridge, MA: Blackwell, 1991); John P. Kotter and L. A. Schlesinger, "Choosing Strategies for Change," *Harvard Business Review,* March/April 1979, pp. 106–114; P. R. Lawrence, "How to Deal with Resistance to Change," *Harvard Business Review,* May/June 1954, pp. 49–57.

17. M. Beer, R. A. Eisenstat, and B. Spector, "Why Change Programs Don't Produce Change," *Harvard Business Review,* November/December 1990, 158–166; R. M. Kanter, *The Change Masters* (New York: Simon & Schuster, 1983); Kurt Lewin, *Field Theory in Social Science* (New York: Harper, 1951). 18.Conner, *Managing at the Speed of Change.*

CHAPTER 3

1. James M. Kouzes and Barry Z. Posner, *The Leadership Challenge* (San Francisco: Jossey-Bass, 1995), p. 29.

2. John P. Kotter, *Leading Change* (Boston: Harvard Business School Press, 1996), p. 72.

CHAPTER 4

1. *The American Heritage Dictionary of the English Language,* New College Edition.

2. David A. Nadler, *Champions of Change: How CEOs and Their Companies Are Mastering the Skills of Radical Change* (San Francisco: Jossey-Bass Publishers, 1998), p. 39.

3. H. Selye, *Stress without Distress* (New York: J B Lippincott, 1974).

4. Jerry W. Gilley and Nathaniel W. Boughton, *Stop Managing, Start Coaching!* (Chicago: Irwin Professional Publishing, 1996).

5. Jerry W. Gilley, Scott A. Quatro, Erik Hoekstra, Doug Whittle, and Ann Maycunich, *The Manager as Change Agent* (Cambridge, MA: Perseus Publishing, 2001), pp. 238–239.

6. A. M. Webber, "Learning for a Change," *Fast Company,* May 1999, p. 180.

7. J. A. Wall Jr. and R. R. Callister, "Conflict and Its Management," *Journal of Management* 3 (1995): p. 517.

8. D. Tjosvold, *Learning to Manage Conflict: Getting People to Work Together Productively* (New York: Lexington Books, 1993), pp. 12–13.

Index

Ability, 36
Accountability, 66
Active listening, 74
Adaptability, 64
Adding value, 68
Adoption, stages of, 23
Alliance builder, 65
Alternatives, 104
Ambiguity, tolerance of, 65
Analysis, steps in, 103–4
Articulateness, 61

Behavior, modeling the, 47
Business acumen, 65
Business and general knowledge, 77

Capabilities and weaknesses, knowledge of, 69
Celebration and rewards, 34
Change, 18, 21, 22; agent, 39; audit, 98–102; barriers to, 11, 13, 67, 98, 106; champions, 14, 40, 50; comprehensive model for, 36, 98, 109; conditions necessary for, 36; coordinating, 49; culture of, 44, 45; developmental, 18, 19; emotional cycle of, 24; environment of, 98, 111; Gilley's 7-step model of, 35; grid, 98, 108; implementation of, 33; Kotter's 8-step model of, 35; Lewin's model of, 34; myths, 18; problems with, 9; processes, 76; reactions to, 22; resistance to, 27, 28, 31, 32; responses to, 30–32; rules of, 37; transitional, 18; transformational, 18; Ulrich's 7-step model of, 35
Change leader, 39, 53, 57; roles and responsibilities of, 39, 41; skills and competencies of, 58–60
Change leadership, 8; action plan for development, 87, 94; characteristics summary, 86–93; purpose of, 4

Change leadership competency questionnaire, 88–94
Change management, 34, 50
Change manager, 40, 41, 49, 53
Coaching, 72
Collaboration, 69
Commitment, 25
Communication, 33, 46, 50, 68; channels, 75; skills, 74; strategic plan, 98, 112
Confidence, 62
Conflict, 51; management of, 76; resistance, plan for, 98, 107; resolution of, 72
Control, 7, 49, 68
Creativity, 63; and innovation, 45
Culture, dysfunctional, 44; organizational, 44

Decision making, 69
Defensive response, 54
Denial, 24
Directing, 7, 49

Early adopters, 23
Early majority, 23
Education and training, 33
Employee involvement, benefits of, 51
Engaging, 63
Evaluation, 69
Expectations, 51
Exploration, 25
External environment, 78

Findings, 104
Flexibility, 71
Foreign body response, 30
Future, imagining the, 40

General knowledge, 78
Generating and assessing alternatives, 70
Giving up, 24, 25
Goals, SMART, 51

Human nature, knowledge of, 71

Immune system, 29; sentinels of the, 30
Informed optimism, 24, 25
Informed pessimism, 24, 25
Innovation, 23; innovators, 23
Inspirer, 40–41, 43
Interaction, two-way, 75
Internal environment, 78
Interpersonal skills, 71
Intrusion, body's response to, 32
Involvement, 33
Involving others, 43, 51; partnering with and, 45

Jaffe, Dennis, 24

Laggards, 23
Late majority, 23
Leadership, 8; skills of, 60
Lewin, Kurt, 34, 97

Macrophages, 30, 31
Management, contemporary, 7, 8; impacts on change, 7; traditional definition of, 49; versus leadership, 5–6
Managers, implications for, 10, 25
Monitoring, 49
Motivation techniques, understanding of, 71
Movement, 34

Negotiation, 77; and coercion, 34

Organizations, 31; resistance to change, 29; responses to change, 32; similarities between the human body and, 31
Organizing, 7, 59, 68

Passion, 61
Perception: negative, 22; positive, 22
Performance management system, 58, 114
Persuasiveness, 61
Plan, 68
Planning, 7, 49

Problem solver, 40, 41, 47, 64
Problem solving, 69
Problems: opportunities or, 104; personal, 51

Recognition and reward, 47, 53
Recommendation(s), 104
Refreezing, 34, 36
Rejection, preventing, 54
Resistance to change: managing, 25; overcoming, 33; symptoms of, 27; understanding causes of, 33
Resources, providing, 45
Reward strategies, 98, 113
Rewarding completion, 24, 25
Risk taker, 61
Rogers, Everett, 23

Sample analysis, 105
Scott, Cynthia, 24
Self-assessment, 85
Self-management, 68
Senge, Peter, 75
Senn, Larry, 24
Situation, analyzing the, 47

Skills: enhancing own, 47; investigative and analytical, 70
Solutions, crafting creative, 48
Status quo, challenging the, 40
Stewardship, philosophy of, 41, 42
Strategy, 64
Strengths and weaknesses, 79
Stress management, 33, 65
Supporter, 40, 41, 44
SWOT analysis, 47, 98, 103

Tjosvold's cooperative conflict model, 77
Training and education, 33
Transformation, 34

Unfreezing, 34–36
Uninformed optimism, 24, 25

Vision, 42; articulating the, 43; shared, 42
Visionary, 40, 41
Visualize, 62

Willingness, 36

About the Author

ANN GILLEY is Associate Professor of Mangement at Ferris State University and Vice President of Trilogy Consulting Group, a performance consulting firm. Formerly on the faculty at Colorado State University, she is co-author of several books, including *The Performance Challenge, Beyond the Learning Organization*, and *Organizational Learning, Performance, and Change*, recipient of the Academy of Human Resources Development book-of-the-year award in 2000.